Adideva
25 Legends behind His 25 Names

Adideva
25 Legends behind His 25 Names

A Yatra through Itihasas, Puranas, and Folklore

Deepa Bhaskaran Salem

ink | OCCAM

First published in India 2024
This edition published 2024

ISBN: 978-93-92209-91-8

BluOne Ink Pvt. Ltd
A-76, 2nd Floor, Sector 136, Noida
Uttar Pradesh 201301
www.bluone.ink
publisher@bluone.ink

ink | OCCAM

To my gurus,
who are none other than Adideva

Contents

List of Figures

Avaṉ aruḷālē avaṉ tāḷ vaṇaṅki

With His own grace, we bow to Him.

—Mānickavāchagar, Tamil poet, 9th century CE

योो गुरुः स शिवः प्रोक्तो यः शिवः स गुरुः स्मृतः ।

The one who is Guru is indeed Siva; the one who is Siva is indeed Guru.

—Guru Gita

A Note to the Readers

Shiva kathas are strewn like bright pearls across the rich, varied, and antiquated treasure chests of our Vedas, Agamas, Tantra Shastras, Itihasas, Maha Puranas, Sthala Puranas, and folklore.

The legends may evoke incredulity even in the devout. They often span vast timelines, highlight extreme powers, traverse great distances, and most of all depict intense emotions including love, passion, anger, compassion, pride, power, and bhakti, or devotion.

It is best to approach them with childlike wonder and complete surrender with the aim of making the stories part of our subconscious. This alone will inspire, purify, and infuse us with bhakti, and lead us to mukti, or liberation.

Like most things in Hindu dharma, the same legends appear in multiple texts with minor and, occasionally, significant differences. In fact, the same story can occur with variations even within the same Purana.

Scholars have attributed these differences to *kalpa bheda*, or the belief that these incidents play out in every kalpa, or cosmic cycle, with nominal variations. These differences can also be attributed to various eyewitness accounts, which then get embellished and altered over time due to the storyteller's unique *rasasvada* (individual appreciation of sentiments and aesthetics).

For instance, the Daksha *yagna* story appears in the *Shiva Purana* in both the Sati Khanda of Rudra Samhita and Vayaveeya Samhita, as also in the Mahabharata Shalya Parva, Devi Bhagavata, and other works. Similarly, the story of the contest for supremacy between Brahma and Vishnu occurs twice within *Shiva Purana*, the first in Vidyeshwara Samhita narrated by Nandikeshwara to Sanatkumara, where Brahma is portrayed in harsh tones, and the second narrated by Brahma himself in the Srshti Khanda of Rudra Samhita, where he paints himself in nobler light.

Where a variant exists, I have mostly chosen the version from the *Shiva Purana.* In a few cases, I have opted to combine details from multiple Puranas for both rasa and the lessons they teach.

The locations of some places are still in doubt. The Nageshwara Jyotirlinga, for example, has three claimants. The Kotirudra Samhita of the *Shiva Purana* indicates it to be near Darukavana, the holy deodar forest, in proximity to the western ocean. There is no such forest near Dwaraka, Gujarat, today, though there is a nearby ocean. Almora in Uttarakhand with its deodar forests could be a possibility, but there is no ocean in the vicinity. The Aundha Nagnath temple in Maharashtra also stakes a claim. There are similar confusions with respect to other locations.

The Sthala Puranas of some temples do not align with the Puranic story. The story of Bhimashankar Jyotirlinga is a case in point. Some episodes that the Sthala Puranas claim are from the Maha Puranas are missing. They are possibly lost or not yet published or translated (for example, the

Sahyadri Khanda of *Skanda Purana*). In such cases, I have relied completely on the *Sthala Puranas* (e.g., *Chidambara Mahatmyam*, *Gajaranya Kshetra Mahatmyam*, and *Srisailam Sthala Purana*).

Modern scholars cast doubt on the authenticity and dating of some Puranas, suggesting that several chapters might be later additions. Such analysis is beyond the scope of this book.

None of these academic calisthenics can divert us from the profound beauty and wonder of Mahadeva kathas.

Introduction
Shiva: Lord of Extreme Contrasts

Who is Shiva? Can one even define him? He is the formless who manifests in myriad forms that defy imagination. Each form is in extreme contrast to another. He represents the contradictions of stillness and energy, austerity and passion, and anger and compassion—he straddles all since he is beyond all.

He is, at the same time,

- the celibate destroyer of Kama and the romantic Kameshwara,
- the primitive hunter Kirata and the evolved Dakshinamurti,
- the dweller of the macabre cemetery and the mesmerizing Kailasha,
- the wrathful Veerabhadra and the benevolent Sadashiva,
- the terrifying Kapalin and the captivating Sundareshwara,
- the lord of the grotesque goblins and the consort of the beautiful Uma,
- the eternally still linga and the dynamic Nataraja.

The gandharva Pushpadanta composed the *Shiva Mahimna Stotram*, describing the grandeur that is Shiva. Struggling to do justice to it, he asserts that even Saraswati cannot succeed in such a task.

asita-giri-samaṃ syāt
kajjalaṃ sindhu-pātrē
sura-taruvara-śākhā
lēkhanī patramurvī ।
likhati yadi gṛhītvā
śāradā sarvakālaṃ
tadapi tava guṇānām
īśa pāraṃ na yāti ॥

Even if we uproot and powder the dark mountain for ink,
And dissolve it in the ocean as the ink pot,
Even if we use a branch of the massive Kalpavriksha tree as pen,
Even if Saraswati Herself writes using
the entire earth as her paper,
She would not be able to completely describe you.

(*Shiva Mahimna Stotram*, verse 32, Pushpadanta)

This inexplicable yet powerful tattva, or truth, of Shiva is infused into the soil of Bharatavarsha. Which village does not have a Shiva temple? Which Indian language does not have a Shiva stuti? Which state does not have Shiva bhaktas meditating on the *panchakshari*?

This book of devotion is a collection of a few enchanting legends about Shiva from the rich lode of Itihasas, Puranas, Sthala Puranas, and folklore. The stories selected are filled with the navarasas and evoke wonder at the tattva that is Mahadeva. They also provide subtle teachings on dharma and adhyatma.

Most importantly, they are the easiest and sweetest way to cultivate Shiva bhakti, which is the immediate cure for samsara.

1
Tripurantaka

Tripura! The name itself evokes size and brilliance akin to cosmic systems. For nearly a millennium, the three colossal cities constructed by Maya, the architect of the *asuras*, for the supremacist brothers Vidyunmali, Tarakaksha, and Kamalaksha traversed the galaxies.

From these cities, the asuric marauders wreaked havoc on the universe, flying in all directions, capturing kings and rishis, erasing civilizations, and incinerating entire planets. Innocents on the earth shuddered from fear of even the sight of these three dazzling bodies in golden, silver, and iron colours. Elders huddled indoors, praying into the night, and mothers quickly covered the eyes of their curious children. A calamity of unimaginable scale loomed over the earth.

Even the most powerful kings and accomplished rishis could not assuage the fear of the people. Helpless, they performed massive yagnas to propitiate the devas and beseech their protection against the impending catastrophe. They offered countless *ahutis*—sacrificial offerings—to the devas.

Agni's normally radiant face began to dim, and he expressed his frustration at Indra's court. "Brothers," he said, "for hundreds of years, we have been gorging on yagna ahutis from humans. They seek our protection from Tripura, yet we are wringing our hands helplessly. I feel embarrassed to accept and bring their offerings to all of you day after day. How long are we going to sit back and do nothing about this terror?"

Indra rubbed his forehead in despair. "Agni, you are not alone. We are helpless. The Tripura brothers have cunningly protected themselves against our best weapons. According to the boon they received, their cities will align once every thousand years for one second, and at that moment, a single arrow must travel across the cosmos and annihilate them. This is beyond our capabilities. My vajra cannot even make a dent."

Brhaspati, the guru of the devas, could not tolerate this fatalism. He calmly reminded them of a possible way out. "Indra, while it is unimaginably difficult, it is not impossible. There is one superpower capable of this task. You all know him. That window of destruction—the time when the cities align—is not far away. Do not miss this opportunity. Seek his help immediately."

Yes, Indra did know who that superpower was. Only, he had been meditating deeply for years. Who would dare to stir him up?

Though petrified of incurring his wrath, the devas rustled up courage and beseeched him. "O Mahadeva, O Karunamurti, the world can no longer bear the torment of these Tripura asuras. The entire universe is overrun by intense fear, but we devas are helpless. Only you can protect us."

Time ticked on intently, waiting for the Lord of Time, Maha Kala, to awaken from his deep penance. The yogi, stirred by the commotion, slowly opened his two reddened eyes to glance at the desperate crowd huddled around him.

Indra heaved a sigh of relief that the fearsome third eye stayed shut.

Mahadeva slowly extended his pillar-like legs, sinews stretching like thick ropes, and stood up tall as a small hillock. His rock-like shoulders heaved as he tightened the rugged elephant skin around his hips. The foamy waters of the Ganga gushed over his massive body. As he swiftly flicked his matted locks, the many snakes slithering on his body lifted their hoods and tightened their hold on his muscled arms. Vasuki, the king of snakes, hissed as his fangs dripped venom involuntarily onto Ishwara's vast chest. Slowly, he opened his mouth, revealing his pearly white teeth. He shaped his right hand into the abhaya mudra and spoke in an ancient voice. "Don't fear."

With his blessing, the devas mobilized. The master architect, Vishwakarma, crafted a celestial chariot that could hurtle through the cosmos like a comet. Brahma served as its charioteer. Hundreds of devas and gandharvas eagerly took the form of horses, pillars, spokes, nails, and axles of the chariot.

The Mandara mountain had once been a churning rod for the milky ocean, and now it became his bow. His trusted snake, Vasuki, became the bowstring. The great Mahavishnu's arrow had Agni seated on the tip and Vayu at the tail end, allowing it to reach its target at lightning speed and burn it up immediately. Every rishi, deva, gandharva, celestial being and earthly power rallied for the impending battle against evil, led by the greatest commander of all times.

As the moment of alignment neared, Shiva ascended the chariot, and the horses sprang forward.

However, the chariot refused to move. The horses strained as Brahma urged them forward. It was of no avail. An ominous crunch resounded through the bewildered silence. The axle, built by the divine architect Vishwakarma, was broken. The dismayed devas stood stunned as the precious seconds ticked away.

Mahadeva frowned, in contemplation, only to erupt in loud laughter, moments later. The devas were disconcerted by Mahadeva's behaviour. Was this the time for hilarity?

Shiva explained, "Did I not declare that all auspicious activities in the universe must begin with the worship of Vighneshwara? But I violated my own rule. Let us pray to him now, before we embark on this war. He will set it right."

His voice reverberated across the cosmos. "Om Gam Ganapataye Namah!" The saptarishis and devas marvelled at the omniscient Lord's submission to dharma and to the promise he made to his son. Their voices rose in unison. "Om Gam Ganapataye Namah!"

Maha Ganapati was tickled by this sight. He roared in laughter, and his *mushika* (his pet mouse) sniggered. With a *hum-kara* (trumpeting sound) from his outstretched trunk, he mended the axle, and the gleaming chariot sprang forth to the skies, hurtling towards Tripura.

Chuckling at his son's lila, Mahadeva lifted his mighty bow just as the three shining cities aligned in space.

With his mighty bow, Shiva aimed at the aligned Tripura cities. The ear-shattering twang of the bow resounded throughout the universe, followed by blinding lights streaking in the far distance. The divine arrow detonated Tripura which shattered into fragments that floated into the vast universe. Some had noticed the Lord playfully lift the bow and release a blazing arrow. Others claimed that he burnt the cities with just a smile. Who can know what exactly happened other than him?

Pushpadanta, the gandharva, pondered if the Lord really needed all this paraphernalia.

Rathaḥ kṣōṇī yantā śatadhṛtiragēndrō dhanurathō
rathāṅgē chandrārkau ratha-charaṇa-pāṇiḥ śara iti |
didhakṣōstē kō'yaṃ tripuratṛṇamāḍambara-vidhiḥ
vidhēyaiḥ krīḍantyō na khalu paratantrāḥ prabhudhiyaḥ ||

When You wanted to burn Tripura, which is akin to a piece of straw to You,
The earth became Your chariot, Brahma Your charioteer,
The great mountain Meru became your bow,
The sun and the moon turned into the wheels,
Vishnu became your arrow.
Did you really need all this paraphernalia, my Lord,
When you are not dependent on them!
(*Shiva Mahimna Stotram*, verse 18, Pushpadanta)

His fame increased exponentially as the Tripurantaka or Tripura Samhara Murti.

Years later, the devas approached Brhaspati with a question that had been plaguing them since that fateful moment of war. "With so much at stake, couldn't the all-powerful Mahadeva have fixed the axle himself?"

Brhaspati smiled. "Shiva is the keeper of truths, satya-sankalpa. His actions must align with his teachings. He mandated the worship of Vighneshwara before undertaking any task. By not being an exception to this rule, he set an example for all of humanity."

While the Thiruvathigai Veerateeshwara temple in Tamil Nadu claims to mark the earthly site of the Tripura battle, the Vigneshwara who broke and subsequently mended the axle is revered at the Achu-muri (axle-breaking) Vinayaka temple in Acharapakkam, Tamil Nadu.

Arunagirinatha, an ardent Kartikeya devotee and brilliant Tamil poet of the 15th century, used this tale to glorify Vinayaka in the very first verse of his magnum opus, *Tirupugazh.*

Muppuram eriseydha acchivan urairatham acchadhu podiseydha athidheera

The chariot axle of Shiva, who burned down Tripura, was shattered by you,
O warrior!

(*Tirupugazh,* verse 1, Arunagirinatha)

While the physical Tripura battle pertains to the cosmic realms, rishis emphasize that Maya, the illusory aspect of Parabrahman, forms our personal Tripuras—our waking, dream, and sleep states. Within them, we gradually expand our egos, harming ourselves and the world.

Shiva, as a guru, offers guidance in dismantling our attachment to our Tripuras. But this transformation occurs only when we seek Ganesha's assistance to overcome the mental obstacles that we face.

Sources: Rudra Samhita, Yuddha Khanda (*Shiva Purana*) and *Acharapakkam Sthala Purana*

The tale of the three cities, Tripura, appears in the Krishna Yajur Veda's Vajasaneyi Samhita, with different versions indicated in the Shatapatha Brahmana and the Taittiriya Samhita. The legend is retold with further elaboration in the Karna Parva of Mahabharata, *Skanda Purana* (Reva Khanda), and *Bhagavata Purana* (7th skandha). Mahadeva is eulogized as Tripurankata in the ancient Tamil Sangam poems (Kalittogai's invocation, for one).

Fig. 1.1 Detailed sculpture of Tripura Samhara at Veerateeswara Temple, Thiruvathigai, Cuddalore, Tamil Nadu. Note the three cities depicted as circles along the right edge, Brahma seated as the charioteer, and the snake Vasuki as the bowstring. While the temple existed even in the 7th century CE, the sculptures are attributed to later Pandyas and Thanjavur Marathas
Photo: Sriram mt (Creative Commons License)

2

Somaskanda

Creation came to an abrupt stop. No mothers cried in labour pain. No eggs hatched. No seed sprouted. Growth, change, and decay across all species came to a standstill.

Panic swept across all worlds and rumours swirled, "Brahma has been imprisoned. There is a new Creator!"

Creation resumed, and the rumours persisted. The rain god Varuna, who had been showering monsoons in the southern plains, claimed to have seen Brahma's water pot and beads, the kamandalu and japa mala, in Kartikeya's possession. He was sitting near the banks of the river Kaveri. Nobody knew why the warrior son of Shiva and Parvati would possess Brahma's crucial paraphernalia. Meanwhile, the Ashwini kumaras, who were returning from Kailasha, reported seeing Brahma imprisoned there.

Concerned, Shiva and Parvati approached Kartikeya. His hand rolling Brahma's japa mala and his mind fixed on the *Pranava*, Kartikeya was intently performing creation, generating beings according to their karmas. Sensing his parents, he opened his eyes and smiled at them.

"Kumara, why are you creating the world? Where is Brahma?" An anxious Parvati asked.

Kartikeya, the boy commander, had been born from Shiva's third eye to become the Deva Senapati, to vanquish a trio of brothers—Surapadma, Simhamukha, and Tarakasura—who had conquered and ravaged the world for 108 yugas.

Kartikeya tilted his head with the righteous defiance of youth and said, "Brahma doesn't deserve to be the creator. He lacks the understanding of the meaning and significance of Pranava." He continued, swirling the japa mala, "I imprisoned him in Kailasha and assumed the role of Creator."

Parvati turned to her Lord, expecting his fiercest anger capable of causing destruction at a cosmic level. To her surprise, there was a wide grin on his face.

"Unpredictable, as usual," she smiled to herself as she sat back to enjoy this father-son lila.

"Dear Skanda," his father approached Kartikeya with proud eyes, "I agree. Brahma should have understood the Pranava before using it to create the worlds. Without accurate and complete knowledge, no task, regardless of its execution, will bear fruit. Yet, jailing him was unwarranted." Kartikeya's young face clouded at his father's disapproval.

Shiva continued, "Do you know the meaning of *Om*?" Kartikeya held his father's gaze, nodding confidently.

Mahadeva smiled and said, "Hmm. In that case, can you explain your understanding of Pranava?" He took a seat on the rock beside his son.

"Swami," the clever son held up his hand, "When I explain the Pranava to you, I am the guru, and you are the shishya. I will explain as a guru, only if you sit below me like a shishya." He pointed to the floor beside his feet.

Parvati trembled, expecting Rudra to erupt in anger at Kartikeya's audacity. But she was surprised yet again as she witnessed the strangest of sights.

Shiva, who is Dakshinamurti, the guru of all gurus, humbly knelt at the feet of his young son and bowed his head in reverence. Parvati watched in wonder at this remarkable brahmopadesha, the teaching of the greatest truths.

All the devas, kinnaras, gandharvas, and rishis marvelled at Mahadeva's humility before his son. Some wizened rishis brushed it off, saying, "We know of incidents where our Lord served even the lowest of humans. This is no big deal."

Persuaded by his parents, Kartikeya released Brahma and restored him to the position of Creator. He gained fame as Swaminatha—the Guru of his Own Father—in the picturesque Swamimalai, one of the six major temples of Muruga in the Tamil region.

The love of a parent overflows when his child excels in wisdom and talent. Mahadeva felt that overwhelming love for Kartikeya and took the form of Somaskanda Murti (sa-Uma-Skanda, with Uma and Skanda).

Adi Shankaracharya described an idyllic, domestic scene of this divine family.

Ihāyāhi vatsēti hastānprasāryā-
hvayatyādarāchChaṅkarē māturaṅkāt।
samutpatya tātaṃ śrayantaṃ kumāraṃ
harāśliṣṭagātraṃ bhajē bālamūrtim ॥

I salute that child who rushed from his mother's lap.
To the embrace of his father Parameshwara's extended arms,
as he lovingly called to him, "Come, my dear son."
(*Subrahmanya Bhujangam*, verse 18, Adi Shankaracharya)

The Somaskanda Murti is said to bless the seeker with the true understanding of the Pranava.

Source: *Swamimalai Sthala Purana*

Fig. 2.1 Somaskanda (Lord Shiva with Uma and Skanda) in bronze, Vijayanagar era, circa 1400 CE (currently in Art Institute of Chicago)

3

Veerabhadra

With Shiva, the Lord of the World, as her husband, adoring her, Sati lacked nothing. The world marvelled at her ability to enchant the ascetic Mahadeva.

All her sisters had married esteemed men chosen by their father, Daksha, including rishis like Kashyapa, Vashishta, and Bhrigu; the handsome Chandra, the moon; and the powerful Yama Dharmaraja. However, Sati was captivated by Shiva, that elusive, majestic yogi of Kailasha. Her father, Daksha Prajapati, had blessed the union, albeit reluctantly.

The couple wandered the Himalayas, enjoying amorous pastimes, telling stories to each other, discussing high philosophy, and during the long afternoons, they even played dice. They cared deeply for creation, and in their joyful togetherness, their compassion overflowed to protect their devotees.

However, there arose discord between this ideal couple, triggered by Daksha's simmering anger toward Shiva.

Once Daksha Prajapati visited the Naimisharanya forest. All the devas and rishis assembled there stood up and saluted him. Mahadeva did not. Daksha perceived this as an insult.

Glaring at Rudra, Daksha raged at the assembled crowd. "All suras and asuras revere me. But this uncouth Rudra, sits back without paying respects to me. No wonder he is savage, accompanied by ghostly ganas. He belongs to the cremation ground, not the yagnashala." Shiva simply smiled mysteriously in response.

Despite knowing about his daughter's conjugal bliss, Daksha's discontent grew into hatred for Shiva. He thought, "While my other sons-in-law are handsome and civilized, this one is an unkempt beggar."

Kapardin: one with matted hair; Kapalin: one with a skull bowl; Gangadhara: one with Ganga on the head; Bhasmaddhulita *vigraha*: one covered in ash; Bhujanga bhushana: one adorned with snakes; Krittivasa: one wearing elephant hide; and Bhutapati: Lord of ghosts and goblins. All these qualities of Mahadeva that his devotees glorified disgusted Daksha.

Daksha did not realize that his son-in-law was beyond beautiful and ugly, civilized and savage, rich and poor, or even good and bad.

Daksha Prajapati organized an opulent yagna, at Kanakhala, on the banks of the Ganga. The architect of the devas, Tvashtr, built magnificent abodes for the esteemed guests. Maharishi Bhrigu organized the *yagnashala* and nominated the priests.

Invitations were sent out to the who's who of the world including saptarishis, devas, vidyadharas, gandharvas, kinnaras, apsaras, and kings. However, one residence did not even get a courtesy invitation—Kailasha.

Nobody spoke up against this intentional exclusion except Dadhichi Maharishi. "O Daksha, it is foolish to not invite Mahadeva. With Shiva, inauspicious things become auspicious. Without Shiva, even auspicious things become inauspicious. Please invite him here."

Daksha laughed derisively at Dadhichi and insulted Shiva further. Unable to hear such slurs, Dadhichi left the yagnashala.

Meanwhile, from the Gandhamadana hill, Sati witnessed her sisters and their families, decked in finery, heading to the yagnashala. On learning about their destination, Sati's eyes widened. She ran to her chamber, teary eyed. Her filial loyalty made her wonder, "Was it an accidental oversight by my father?"

She attempted to do what all wise women do in their families—soften emotions, mollify anger, chisel egos, counsel gently, build bridges, and create harmony. She was both a pativrata who wanted due respect for her husband and a caring daughter who wanted to drive sense into her deluded father.

She went to Shiva and said, "You are Yagnapati, the Lord of Sacrifices. How can a yagna happen without you? Let us go." She implored him. He refused, saying, "Dakshayani, your filial attachment is making you overlook the facts. I will not go where I am not welcome. Go, if you wish to."

She went to the yagnashala to change her father's mind. Arriving at the bustling yagnashala, she advised, pleaded with, and finally threatened Daksha. "Father, you may not like Shiva as a son-in-law, but you cannot ignore him as the Lord of yagnas. Not only will your yagna be unfruitful without Sadashiva but it will definitely have the opposite effect. Invite him now and avert a catastrophe."

Daksha scoffed at her arguments. "Your beggar husband with his savage clothes, ash-covered body, and skull bowl will pollute my yagna. He is not welcome here!"

As she turned to the devas and the scholarly rishis for advocacy, they shifted nervously, avoiding her eyes. Appalled and insulted, Sati contemplated leaving the yagnashala. But she feared facing Shiva.

She squeezed her eyes shut. Her name, Dakshayini, felt like a curse as it was associated with her father. Her exquisite face contorted with revulsion at inhabiting the body that was born from Daksha.

She invoked her *jataragni*, the yogic inner fire, and allowed the flames to consume her body. The universe lurched into chaos at this disturbance in Shakti. Ill omens spread across the world. The rishis foresaw massive calamities. Despite the death of his own daughter and the laments of his wife, Daksha commanded the priests to purify the yagnashala and proceed with the yagna.

Back in Kailasha, this tragedy caused unprecedented disturbance in Mahadeva's *tapas.* His eyes flew open as he divined the occurrence. The one who could not be disturbed was disturbed. The unshakable was shaken. He cried out for Sati, his life and breath.

A vivid red seeped into his countenance, his eyes shown bloodshot with rage and grief. His voice rose to a ululation that thundered across the world. "Dak…sha…

yi…neeee….” His ganas watched in horror as he ran mad across the Himalayas. Glaciers sprang where his feet fell. Forests burned, ignited by his anger. Animals ran from their habitats in the face of massive earthquakes.

Nandikeshwara, in an attempt to calm Mahadeva, played his mridangam vigorously. First sporadically and then rhythmically, Rudra's feet transitioned from their mad run into the tandava dance. Nandi then slowed down his rhythm, guiding the Lord of Dance to ease into a sober stop.

His blind rage now gave way to decisive action. Sati must be avenged. The guests at Daksha's yagnashala must be punished for their cowardice.

Mahadeva plucked a hair from his matted locks and flung it on the mountain floor. An enormous crack formed, and out sprang two majestic and formidable beings, Veerabhadra and Bhadrakali, the male and female embodiments of Mahakala's righteous anger.

Hordes of bhutas and pretas, the ghost and goblin followers of Mahadeva, the Navadurgas and their shakti army, followed this duo. They raided Daksha's yagnashala, where a gory battle ensued. The Adityas couldn't match the savage rage of Shiva's army. The Shiva ganas flung them far, dug out the eyes of Bhaga, and smashed the teeth of Pusha. The great Mahavishnu was stunned by the fury of Veerabhadra. He left with Brahma, convinced that Daksha was in the wrong. Veerabhadra made his way to Daksha and dealt the final blow by severing his head from his body.

However, this immediate retribution could not soothe Shiva's overwhelming grief. He let out a bloodcurdling scream at the sight of Sati's burnt body. The devas and rishis wondered how the greatest *vairagi*, the most dispassionate being, could behave like a besotted human. They mistook his vairagya as absence of emotions, while in fact, Mahadeva is the storehouse of all emotions.

He flung Sati's corpse over his shoulders and continued his devastating Rudra Tandava, the dance of anger, which could lead to *pralaya*, the catastrophic dissolution of the universe. Mahavishnu, the preserver of Creation, decided to step in. He flung his Sudarshana Chakra, slicing Sati's body into pieces and dispersed them across the world. Each sliver became a shakti peetha that pulsated with her divinity. They attracted great devotees who built temples in her honour, invoking her shakti.

Shiva fell back into a deep samadhi. No one could awaken him for eons. It necessitated Sati's rebirth as Parvati who would spark him back to the drama of the universe and lead to Kumara sambhavam, the birth of Kartikeya.

Meanwhile, the terrifying Veerabhadra manifestation came to be worshipped by many across Bharata and other Buddhist lands. Aghoris worshipped him as Bhairava. Indian villagers sought his protection in many forms, ranging from Aiyyanar, Bijat Maharajah, Panjurli to Karuppannasami. The Kashmir Shaivas consider Bhairava as Parabrahman, the supreme power itself.

The most powerful form of Veerabhadra with eight arms carries a *trishula* (trident), *khadga* (sword), *pinaka* (bow), deer (indicating the restless mind), and *kapala* (the skull, indicating the ego). Often, he is followed by a dog, which indicates dharma and is surrounded by the *bhuta-ganas.*

Sources: Kedara Khanda (*Skanda Purana*); Santi Parva (Mahabharata); and *Shiva Purana*

4

Uma Maheshwara

A resplendent, royal maiden was exhibiting strange behaviour, discarding her silken attire for a coarse bark robe. As her companions watched in confused panic, she yanked off her golden necklaces, earrings, and bangles, and threw them on the floor. She undid the elaborate arrangement of her long, black tresses and rolled them up into a top knot.

Thus transformed, her face assumed a mask of stern resolve. She ran down the stairs of the palace and out in the direction of the forest. Her elderly mother stood there sobbing helplessly.

Mena had cherished her daughter Parvati's beauty since her birth. All mothers delight in dressing up their daughters and watching them grow into charming ladies. With a daughter whose beauty would captivate the three worlds, Mena surpassed them all. She sought out the best silks, ordered the most exquisite jewellery, and experimented with unique hairdos to further enhance her daughter's ethereal beauty. Mena's attachment to her daughter's external appearance became excessive.

Mena's mind was shrouded by fear as she contemplated her daughter's future. Ever since Narada Muni had planted an admiration for Shiva in her, Parvati had insisted on marrying only that Adiyogi. Mena was appalled by Shiva's appearance and lifestyle. She could not suffer such a grotesque man to stand next to her elegant daughter.

Her disapproval ran deeper still. Shiva's home was a barren ridge in Kailash. His servants were terrifying. His antics were unpredictable. She feared that he would be a terrible husband for her sweet daughter, failing to provide a deserving life for one so gently raised.

She shuddered. Then, her brows smoothened slightly. Since the tragic loss of Sati, Shiva was a sworn celibate. She did not expect him to accept Parvati. She hoped that her foolish girl would return, rejected, and regretting her choice, would agree to marry a handsome, gentle prince of her parents' choosing. She walked back into her chamber, reminiscing about Parvati's birth.

In their youth, Mena and her husband, Himavan, king of the mountains, had performed intense penance to Adi Parashakti seeking her as their child. Eventually, a captivating child was born to them. But Mena did not realize that her prayers had been answered and that Adi Parashakti had indeed been born to them, as Parvati. If she had, she would have realized that it was impossible to keep Parvati away from Shiva.

Besides, their union was critical for the universe. There was a new menace thriving in the shadows. It was Tarakasura. Intent on cosmic supremacy and armed with powerful boons from Brahma, Taraka had already vanquished the devas.

He had imprisoned Indra's son Jayanta and threatened the honour and lives of the deva women.

Lamenting their plight, the devas secretly assembled at Brahmaloka.

A guilt-ridden Brahma avoided their gaze. "Tarakasura has outwitted me. They asked me for a boon that only a son born to Shiva can vanquish them. And I unthinkingly consented to their request. However, after the tragic end of Sati, Shiva has taken an unshakeable vow of celibacy. How can we expect a son from him?"

The sublime environs of Kailasha which had resonated with the music and laughter of Sati, the profound philosophical discussions between Sati and Shiva, and their lila were now bereft of all joy. Since her disappearance, Mahadeva had submerged into yogic samadhi for years.

Brahma proposed a solution. "Adi Parashakti has incarnated as Parvati, the daughter of Himavan. Only she can draw Mahadeva out of his celibacy. Let Narada plant the seed of desire for Shiva in Parvati and let us hope she invokes love in his heart," he sighed.

Narada was dispatched. For him, it was a sweet task to eulogize Mahadeva and convince Parvati that Shiva was her destiny. He suggested that she devote herself to Mahadeva's service.

Himavan and Mena were sceptical about this match, the latter especially so. Narada convinced them. "This is a match you can never prevent. And it is a match most auspicious for the world. A love like theirs will not be found anywhere, neither in the past nor in the future."

Himavan took the smitten Parvati to introduce her to Mahadeva, who was performing his penance in Gangavatarana, a Himalayan ridge where the mighty Ganga sprung from.

"Mahadeva, we are blessed you have chosen this serene spot for your meditation. It will also be my honour if you allow my daughter and her companions to serve you. It is her intense desire to do so," Himavan pleaded.

Shiva's eyes, red shot after a long period of meditation, descended on the beautiful Parvati. Unmoved by such beauty he said, "A woman is of no use to me, an ascetic. Women only bring *prakrti*—wordliness. That prakrti is unreal and can destroy penance. Take her away."

Himavan hesitated to respond, so Parvati chimed in.

"O Yogi, your logic is flawed. You say you do not want prakrti. Yet even your penance is prakrti. What you eat, hear, and speak are all prakrti. To say prakrti is unreal is incorrect. How can you avoid it?" She countered using the Sankhya philosophical view.

Secretly admiring her wisdom and courage, Shiva conceded and allowed Parvati to serve him. What followed were delightful days for Parvati.

She washed his feet, refreshed the *kusha* grass he sat on, brought sacrificial wood for him, and strung flower garlands for him to wear. Through it all, her eyes feasted on him with increasing devotion. He too observed her committed service and control of the senses.

Time, the reliable magician, would have caused their union eventually. But the devas lacked patience. Their suffering forced them to attempt to expedite this process.

On Brahma's advice, Indra called Kama, the love god. "Kama, the union of Shiva and Parvati is inevitable. However, despite their physical proximity, their love story is not progressing. Only you can hasten their union, thereby facilitating our rescue from the asura."

The purpose of Kama's existence was to ignite love. He had every tool at his disposal to do so. Supported by his wife, Rati, he infused spring into Gangavatarana. The cold, barren landscape transformed into a tropical paradise filled with fragrant flowers on which bees buzzed. Ashoka and mango trees flowered, attracting chirping birds. Animals started their mating calls. Even the ascetics meditating there could not escape the amorous instincts.

Having created this perfect environment for love, Kama stood behind Shiva, invisible, waiting to release his Harshana arrow from his sugarcane bow. That arrow could ignite the most romantic passion in the heart it entered. Brahma and the devas watched from afar.

Parvati was especially entrancing that day. Her heart swelled with love, her body ached for his embrace, and her eyes drooped in uncharacteristic languor.

As Parvati prostrated to him and offered flowers at his feet, Shiva saw her with new eyes. Kama's arrow had hit its mark. The celibate Shiva found himself thinking of how pleasurable it would be to embrace her.

It was but a fleeting thought. But the great Yogi recognized this minute disturbance in his mind. As Shiva wondered how lustful thoughts could have entered his mind, he sensed Kama behind him. He turned his enraged gaze on the god of love. He opened his fearsome third eye—the source of annihilation of the universe during pralaya, the great dissolution.

Before anybody could intervene, his *netragni*, fire from his third eye reduced Kama to ashes. Brahma and the devas were aghast. Kama's wife, Rati, fainted in shock.

As Shiva's anger cooled, the devas and Brahma pleaded to him. "O Compassionate One, this is not Kama's fault. We asked him to ignite your attraction to Parvati—not for any frivolous cause but to help vanquish Tarakasura. We beseech you to restore Kama for the sake of the world."

A calmer Mahadeva prophesied Kama's rebirth on earth as Krishna's son, Pradyumna. Until then, he would exist without a body.

In all this commotion, nobody noticed Parvati. Embarrassed by her own lustful feelings, confused by his harsh rejection, and panicked by his sudden wrath, she ran back home. The subsequent days were spent in a daze, consumed by thoughts of Shiva, lamenting their separation, and worrying about her future.

While Himavan was concerned, Mena was relieved. "Parvati will come out of this stupor," she reassured herself. Yet, days passed, and Parvati showed no interest in life. Only the name of Sadashiva ran through her heart like a steady stream. Unconsciously, the name would escape her lips in a whisper, "Shiva… Shiva…"

Narada soon visited her to continue his mission of uniting the couple. Gazing at Parvati's distraught face, he counselled, "Parvati, a lot has happened. It is natural to be confused and distressed. Yet, your marriage to Shiva is destined. Do not give up. He can be attained through devotion and penance. Let me initiate you in the Panchakshari mantra. Immerse yourself in it until he accepts you."

On receiving the initiation of the mantra, a clarity arose in Parvati's troubled heart. Penance, alone, could help her achieve what physical beauty or material offerings could not. Resolute, she approached her parents to seek their permission to leave for the forests to perform her penance. Himavan was accepting of her wishes, but Mena disagreed.

"Is it not enough that you went to serve Shiva and returned broken? Why must a young girl perform penance in the forest? Why should Mahadeva demand that? Do not U-ma!" Despite her best efforts, Mena could not weaken Uma's resolve. She watched helplessly as her daughter transformed from a royal princess into an austere ascetic and departed with a quick prostration to her parents.

Finding a serene spot in the Shringitirtha, Parvati commenced her penance. In her single-minded goal to attain the One, the young girl forgot her senses. The elements did not affect her. Her mind existed beyond the cycle of time. In the first year, she subsisted on wild fruits. In her second year, she lived merely on leaves. Years passed and she gave up eating that too, earning the name Aparna.

Time stopped for her. The Panchakshari mantra resonated from every pore of her emaciated body. Countless sages, devas and gandharvas came to marvel at her. Their hearts emptied of negativity in her presence. Even wild animals folded their limbs and sat silently near their prey.

Parvati did not put a time limit on her penance, but her parents were distressed by her pitiful state. They begged her to stop. "Mahadeva is devoid of emotion. Why else would he put you through such a torturous penance? Just as the moon cannot be caught, Shiva also cannot be attained. Give up, Uma."

Her resolve remained unwavering. "I have taken a vow and will not give up without accomplishing it. Sadashiva will honour my penance. I have no doubt." Her eyes closed and her mind was absorbed back into Panchakshari. Himavan and Mena trudged back home, filled with misgivings.

As her penance intensified, her yogic shakti spread across the universe, scorching it with its intensity. Panicked, Brahma and the devas ran to Mahavishnu. He advised them to appeal to Shiva to put an end to Parvati's tapas.

They all eulogized him until he opened his eyes. Vishnu explained the situation with Taraka and the disturbance due to Parvati's penance. Could Mahadeva not marry the virtuous Parvati? Could he not accede to the wishes of the devas and beget a son to vanquish Taraka?

Mahadeva resisted. "Kama is the root of all conflict in the world. If I marry Parvati, Kama will rise again and disturb the serenity of all sadhus." Shiva continued to extol the benefits of celibacy and sannyasa. The devas and Mahavishnu felt helpless in the face of this sermon.

The ever-compassionate Shiva continued, "Yet, I will marry Parvati for your sake. Let us first test her commitment. Ask the Saptarishis—the seven sages—to try and stop her penance."

The Saptarishis went on this errand and soon returned, conceding failure. They were unable to shake Parvati's love for Shiva. "She not only adores you, Lord, but she has a clear understanding of who you are. She knows you as Brahman, the unchanging, devoid of names and forms. She does not care for your outer appearance or ornaments. To be honest, we all wish for your union."

Shiva pondered, "Does she truly know and love me, as the Saptarishis claim? I will test her myself."

He appeared before her as an aged brahmana as she was preparing to intensify her tapas with fire. As she prostrated to him, he enquired about the reason for her penance.

Upon learning of her intention to marry Shiva, he roared with laughter. "Shiva? For you, gentle maiden? Do you know of him? Let me educate you." He circled Parvati, showering insults upon Shiva. "He is hideous in appearance, matted hair locks dancing on his shoulders, ash smeared all over his naked body, a tattered elephant skin hanging from his hip and snakes encircling his neck. He owns nothing but skulls and bulls. His companions are goblins and ghosts. His behaviour is unpredictable. He dances violently, drinks poison, and goes into samadhi or erupts in anger without warning."

He would have continued with his poetic insults for the great Lord but was interrupted by Parvati. She was livid. "Stop! I would have killed you for such nonsense if only you weren't an aged brahmana. You know nothing of the Lord. I cannot suffer your presence any longer." As she was marching off from that place, she found herself embraced from behind.

She turned around in panic only to be met with the Lord of her heart, in the place of the brahmana. Immeasurable joy and relief flooded into her. All the agony from years of penance evaporated in that moment.

"Parvati, you are my wife for eternity. Your intelligence, your grace and your devotion has enamoured me. Come with me to my abode." Shiva held out his hand, smiling.

Uma brought her palms together. "Lord, as Sati, I believe my marriage to you did not last because the rites were left incomplete. This time, let us marry following all the vivaha rituals and the blessings of the rishis. I know you are beyond all conventions, but please request for my hand from my father."

Acquiescing, Shiva departed. Parvati rushed back home with the wonderful news only to meet her parents' mixed reactions. They were relieved that she had returned, but Mena was still reluctant about the match.

Mahadeva enacted a series of lilas to win them over. He first appeared as a dancing beggar and then as a mendicant, seeking Parvati as a gift. Tricked by his disguises, Himavan and Mena refused.

Rishi Vashishta intervened. He advised Himavan, "Shiva is testing you. Do not fall for his tricks. Accept him not only as the Supreme Lord, but as the inevitable groom for your daughter." Vashishta's wife, Arundhati, too tried to alleviate Mena's concerns.

Himavan was ashamed. "I have learnt my lesson. I surrender everything I possess to Shiva for he is the Lord of everything, not just a mendicant. Let us fix the wedding date."

Sadashiva was satisfied and ordered the wedding preparations to proceed.

Himavan organized a wedding unlike anything anybody had witnessed before. Vishwakarma built the mantapa in a place called Triyuginarayan. Great yagnas were performed. Waters were fetched from the sacred rivers. The entire settlement was decorated. Guest houses were built to accommodate countless visitors. Mesmerizing music resounded and delectable foods were served.

On the auspicious day, a small miracle happened in Kailasha. Shiva allowed the seven mothers—the Sapta Matrikas—to style him for the wedding. His ornaments transformed him into Sundareshwara, the captivating one.

His moon recast itself as a crown. His third eye appeared as a jewel on his forehead. The serpents changed into glittering jewels. The ash on his body gave out a sweet fragrance. The elephant hide shone like yellow silk. He looked enchanting, like the storehouse of the entire world's wealth and charm.

Brahma and the rishis started the rituals following the shastras. The wedding procession started its journey to Oshadhiprastha, the capital of Himavan's kingdom. It stretched for miles—Vishnu, Brahma, devas, gandharvas, rishis, ganas and their entourage sang and danced strewing flowers and beating drums. At the end of this parade was Sundareshwara seated on a pristine, white bull.

Before the wedding, more lila was in the offing. Any remnant of scepticism had to be removed from Mena's mind before the union.

As they neared Himavan's palace, Mena was curious to see her prospective son-in-law. Was he truly as great as Narada and the rishis eulogized? Was he as handsome as Parvati described? She stepped onto the balcony to observe. Narada joined her there.

Hordes of handsome men—Indra, Varuna, Vishnu, Gandharvas, Yakshas—walked by. Mena thought each handsome man to be Shiva, but Narada corrected her.

Mena was convinced that Shiva, who had such handsome and elegant friends, must himself show like a priceless jewel amongst his beautiful peers.

After a long wait, Narada pointed out. "That, on that white bull, is Mahadeva, your son-in-law."

Mena was aghast. Her eyes did not see the richly dressed, handsome Lord. She saw his usual form smeared with ash, snakes, animal skin and matted hair. Terrified by the Lord's illusion, Mena fainted. On regaining consciousness, she lamented.

"What a wretched day for my daughter! You have tricked her into falling for such an uncouth man. I will never give my daughter to such a repulsive groom." She raged against Brahma, Narada, and the rishis.

Her husband Himavan rushed to her. "O Mena, come out of your delusion. What kind of a mother behaves like this at their daughter's wedding? You still have not understood Shiva."

The gods and rishis convinced her that Shiva looked grotesque to her alone. Mena was taken aback. "Is that so? Let him show me his lovely form. Otherwise, I will not give him my daughter." She crossed her arms and stood firm.

The procession drew closer. And then Mena's eyes opened wide, and her pupils dilated. Her body shook, struggling to take in this vision.

His exquisite form radiated like a thousand suns. His skin shone white as camphor. His broad forehead and sharp nose were majestic. His lips, red as a *bimba* fruit, curved in a captivating smile. His luxuriant hair glistened on his shoulders and his muscles rippled on his long limbs and wide torso. His dazzling ornaments and silken garments only served to enhance his beauty. His eyes, large as lotus petals, twinkled in humour as he gazed back at her. "Am I handsome, rich, and civilized enough for your daughter now?" they seemed to taunt her.

Mena stammered, unable to articulate her surprise and relief. "Parvati is wise, indeed. Wiser than me that she saw his true beauty even without the outer adornments."

All hurdles overcome, the wedding proceeded with grand rituals and enthusiastic participation. Amid sonorous Vedic chants and auspicious music, Shiva clasped Parvati's delicate hand. She became Shivani, Bhavani, Sharvani and Maheshwari through their union. And he proudly embraced the new epithets of Parvati Pati, Gowri Shankara, and Uma Maheshwara.

Their love for each other nourished the universe. Kama was revived and led to countless human unions. Peace descended upon the minds of rishis. Joy flowed through the devas' minds. Their son, Kumara, also known as Kartikeya, would soon be born.

This grand union has great philosophical and religious significance. However, the sheer joy of reliving this love story has driven countless poets to retell it in all its glory.

Kalidasa immortalizes it in his Kumara Sambhavam with sweet, vivid descriptions. Bhagavan Adi Shankaracharya revels in worshipping them as one.

Namaḥ śivābhyāṃ navayauvanābhyāṃ
parasparāśliṣṭavapurdharābhyām
nagēndrakanyāvṛṣakētanābhyāṃ
namō namaḥ śaṅkarapārvatībhyām

I bow to God Shiva and Goddess Parvathi (Shivaa),
who are eternally young,
who embrace each other affectionately.
The beloved daughter of the Mountain,
the Lord carrying a bull flag.
I bow to you, again and again,
God Shiva and Goddess Parvati.
(*Uma Maheshwara Stotram*, Adi Shankaracharya)

Sources: Rudra Samhita, Parvati Khanda (*Shiva Purana*) and Maheshwara Khanda and Kedara Khanda (*Skanda Purana*)

Brief mentions are in *Brahma Purana*, *Devi Bhagavata Purana* and Swargarohana Parva (*Mahabharata*). Kalidasa dramatizes this episode in his *Kumara Sambhavam.*

Fig. 4.1 Kalyanasundara, the wedding of Shiva and Uma, with Brahma as the presiding priest. Ellora Caves, Maharashtra, 6th century CE, Kalachuri Dynasty

5

Ardhanarishwara

The great Rishi Bhringi was a devout Shiva bhakta. In addition, he played the role of dance master for his Lord Nataraja's incomparable dances. Adi Shankaracharya highlights Bhringi's great fortune while describing the Lord:

bhṛngīchchā-naṭanōtkaṭaḥ

The One who dances to Bhringi's desire.
(*Shivanandalahari*, verse 51, Adi Shankaracharya)

Yet, blinded by his Shiva bhakti, he refused to bow down to anyone else, including Devi Parvati. Every day, he would worship and circumambulate Mahadeva in Kailasha, but would pointedly ignore Devi.

Tired of this fanaticism, Parvati wanted to teach Bhringi a lesson. Shiva advised her to ignore it. He said, "Devi, are you separate from me? I consider your worship to be my worship. Is my worship then, not synonymous to yours?" But Parvati was determined to make a point.

The next morning, Rishi Bhringi found Parvati seated firmly on Shiva's lap, convinced that this arrangement would force Bhringi to prostrate before her. She had underestimated Bhringi's ingenuity. Utilizing his *siddhis*, powers attained through his penance, Bhringi transformed into a snake, slithering around Shiva to perform his parikrama. Parvati, though taken aback, remained steadfast in her resolve.

She then asked Shiva for a boon to share his body and become half of it. Shiva joyfully granted her the boon, and the mesmerizing form of Ardhanarishwara, half-woman and half-man manifested to the amazement of all.

Rishi Bhringi was not ready to concede defeat. This time, the sage turned into a beetle, drilled a hole through Ardhanarishwara, and circumambulated only the male half.

Parvati, enraged by his defiance, cursed Bhringi, declaring he would lose the parts of his body derived from his mother. Instantaneously, Rishi Bhringi's muscles began pouring out of his body, leaving him a skeletal mass. As he was about to collapse, Shiva intervened, granting him an additional leg for support.

Despite her frustration, Parvati could not help but marvel at the muni's unwavering devotion. Rishi Bhringi acknowledged his immaturity in trying to separate Shakti from Shiva, recalling the truth about their inseparable union.

Shakti is the life force of Shiva. Without her, Shiva is a mere Shava, a corpse. She embodies the iccha-shakti, krya-shakti, and jnana-shakti of Shiva—the power of motivation, action, and knowledge of Shiva, the unchanging, causeless brahman.

Adi Shankaracharya puts this poetically as he launches his famous *Soundarya Lahari*.

Śivaḥ śaktyā yukto yadi bhavati śaktaḥ prabhavitum |
na cedevam devo na khalu kuśalaḥ spanditum api ||

With Shakti, Shiva is endowed with the
power to create the universe.
Without her, he is incapable of even the slightest movement.
(*Saundaryalahiri*, verse 1, Adi Shankaracharya)

She is glorified across Bharata in infinite forms: the Maya of Vedanta, the Mula Prakriti of Sankhya, the Parabrahman of the Shaktas, Devi Lalitha Tripurasundari of Tantra, Shiva's consort for the Shaivas, Mahavishnu's sister for the Vaishnavas, the leader Durga of the shaktis, the dashamahavidyas and the yoginis, Shitala, or Mariamman of the villagers, and so on. Her stories are as vast and varied as His.

Yet, He and She are not separate. The unmanifest consciousness, Shiva, manifests in this world through his intrinsic Shakti, an exquisite interplay of masculine and feminine that remains indivisible from Shiva.

Mahakavi Kalidasa's renowned prayer verse in the great *Raghuvamsha Mahakavya* is the pinnacle of poetic brilliance, depicting this divine couple, the cosmic progenitors.

Vāgarthāviva sampruktau vāgarthapratipattaye
jagataḥ pitarau vande pārvatīparameśvarau

To understand words and their meanings,
I worship Parvati and Parameshwara, the parents of the world,
who are both inseparable like a word and its meaning.
(*Raghuvamsha*, Kalidasa)

He examines their relationship. Are they like typical spouses? No, their connection defies dissolution, unlike modern marriages. Known as a master of similes, the poet likens their connection to the link between a word and its meaning. Kalidasa asserts that they can only be accessed together—a lesson Bhringi learnt.

The revered Maharashtrian saint Jnaneshwara also strives to capture this beautiful oneness that appears as two.

jeNeM deveM saMpUrNa devI |
jiyeviNa kAMhIMnA to gosAvI |
kiMbahunA ekopajIvI |
eka_ekAMchI || 1\-10||
kaisA meLu AlA goDiye |
doghe na mAtI jagIM iye |
kIM paramANUhi mAjI uvAye |
mAMDilIM AhAtI || 1\-11||
jihIM eka_ekAvINa |
na kIje tR^iNAcheMhI nirmANa |
jiye doghe jIvaprANa | jiyA doghA || 1\-12||

Because of God, the Goddess exists, and without her, he is not.
They exist only because of each other!
How sweet is their union?
Two lutes, one note
Two flowers, one fragrance
Two lamps: one light
Two lips, one word
Two eyes, one sight
These two: One universe
(*Amritanubhava*, Jnaneshwara)

Shiva's physical attributes, ornaments, and weapons on the right and Devi's on the left make Ardhanarishwara a fascinating iconography, the earliest of which is a Kushana torso in Mathura estimated to be of 1 CE, demonstrating how ancient this form is. Often, their vahanas, Nandi, or the bull, and Simha, or the lion, appear on their respective sides.

The *Ardhanarishwara Stotram*, composed by Bhagavan Adi Shankara, revels in their dance, which encompasses the creation, destruction, and regeneration of the world.

Prapañcasṛṣṭyun mukhalāsyakāyai samastasaṃhāraka tāṇḍavāya
jagajjananyai jagadekapitre namaḥ śivāyai ca namaḥ śivāya | |

My salutations to both Parvathi and Shiva,
To Her, whose dance marks the creation of the world,
To Him, whose dance destroys everything,
To Her, who is the mother of the universe,
To Him, who is the father of the universe.
(*Ardhanarishwara Stotram*, verse 7, Adi Shankaracharya)

The meditative form of Ardhanarishwara can lead us to a vision of their Oneness.

Source: *Sthala Purana* of Virupaksha Temple, Hampi, Karnataka

Fig. 5.1 Ardhanarishwara torso in a Kushana period stele, circa 35–60 AD. Currently in Government Museum, Mathura

Source: http://picasaweb.google.com/injamaven

6

Dakshinamurti

The Sanatkumaras were repulsed. Their quest for the supreme knowledge of the Self, Brahma Vidya, had led them to Vaikuntha to seek Mahavishnu as their guru. There they chanced upon a vision of Vishnu reclining languidly in his snake mattress with his consort, Mahalakshmi, massaging his feet. They wondered how the highest knowledge, requiring complete detachment, could be gained from one so openly indulged in luxury.

The four Kumaras were the manasa putras—mind-born sons—of Brahma. The creator expected them to populate the world through marriage and procreation. As soon as they were born, he exposed them to the philosophy of the Vedas. Impacted by its teachings, the four young boys immediately lost all interest in material life and decided to focus on gaining self-realization.

After years of tapas, they had developed intense concentration and renounced all shred of desire. They soon realized the need for a guru to guide them to enlightenment. And that need had brought them to Vaikuntha, where they faced this disappointing sight.

So, they decided to turn to their own father. A similar spectacle awaited them at Brahmaloka. Melodic music emanated from Devi Saraswati's famed string instrument, the veena, as Brahma sat there immersed in the sensory experience of the music. The Kumaras doubted whether their father, so taken by sensory pursuits, could truly be a realized master. They rejected Brahma as their guru.

Their sole remaining option was Kailasha. Sadashiva was known as the greatest vairagi, one without desires. One who drank poison and wore *bhasma* would surely be beyond sensual temptations. Eager to attain Shiva's guidance, they bypassed Nandikeshwara at the gates of Kailasha and marched into its inner realms. A tremendous shock awaited them.

Sadashiva had surpassed even Vishnu and Brahma in his sensual pursuits. The Sanatkumaras found Uma seated on Shiva's lap, being lustfully caressed by her husband. They stopped at the door, dumbstruck. Before the divine couple could acknowledge them, they turned on their heels and rushed out of Kailasha as though that mere sight had scorched them.

Puzzled by their behaviour, Uma turned to her Lord. "Why did the Kumaras run away like Kailasha was on fire? Did we upset them somehow?"

Sadashiva divined the reason. "Uma, the Kumaras are seeking a realized guru to teach them the truth about the Atman. However, erroneously, they believe that a guru must be in perpetual meditation, renouncing all else. They need to be taught the truth."

He assumed the form of a youthful brahmachari, shining with brilliance. He reached the forest of the Sanatkumaras and sat down under a huge banyan tree, facing the south. With his eyes closed in meditation, his right hand formed the chin-mudra.

The troubled Sanatkumaras lamenting the difficulty of finding the right guru felt themselves being drawn to the banyan tree, which shown with an inexplicable radiance. As if pulled by magic, they sat reverentially at the feet of the tranquil youth under the tree and gazed at his chin-mudra.

Days passed. No sound emanated from the youthful guru or the aged shishyas. Despite the absence of verbal exchange, clarity dawned within their minds.

Chitraṃ vaṭatarōrmūlē vṛddhāḥ śiṣyāḥ gururyuvā ।
gurōstu maunavyākhyānaṃ śiṣyāstuchChinnasaṃśayāḥ ॥

It is a strange sight under a banyan tree.
Old disciples with a young teacher
The teacher teaches in silence.
Yet the students have had their doubts cleared.
(*Dakshinamurthi Dhyana Stotram*)

The chin-mudra unveiled profound insights. The middle, ring, and little fingers represented the three states of waking, dreaming, and deep sleep; the index finger signified the *jeevatma*, the individual; and the independent thumb indicated the *paramatma*, the eternal Brahman.

The Sanatkumaras realized that the jeevatma, as the individual, aligns itself with the waking, dream, and sleep states, going through the entire spectrum of experiences, over multiple births, just as the index fingers operate along with the three middle, ring, and little fingers. However, the turning of the index finger to join the thumb, portrayed the unity of the jeevatma and the paramatma, unaffected by the three states (the three other fingers).

Understanding this metaphor, the Sanatkumaras grasped that the atman remains untouched by the actions of the body and mind in the waking, dreaming, and sleep states. Vishnu relaxing, Brahma enjoying music, or Sadashiva consorting with his wife would not taint the ever-pure, ever-auspicious, ever-conscious atman.

Adi Shankaracharya captured with exquisite clarity that a realized person is in bliss whether he is in yoga (meditation) or bhoga (enjoyment) with people or alone.

Yōgaratō vā bhōgaratō vā saṅgaratō vā saṅgavihīnaḥ ।
yasya brahmaṇi ramatē chittaṃ nandati nandati nandatyēva ॥ *20* ॥

Whether in yoga or bhoga, whether in company or alone,
For one whose mind revels in Brahman, it is bliss,
bliss, and only bliss.
Bhaja Govindam (*Moha Mudgaram*), Adi Shankaracharya

Thus, Dakshinamurti became the guru of all gurus, the Adi guru, initiating the endless Guru Parampara, the line of masters, who have passed down this knowledge through generations.

Nidhayē sarvavidyānāṃ bhiṣajē bhavarōgiṇām ।
guravē sarvalōkānāṃ dakṣiṇāmūrtayē namaḥ ॥

Salutations to that Dakshinamurti,
The teacher of the entire world,

The healer of the disease of the birth–death cycle,
The storehouse of all knowledge
(*Dakshinamurti Dhyana Stotram*)

Dakshinamurti is seated in Shiva temples facing south, resting his feet on Apasmara Purusha, a dwarf symbolizing our ignorance-filled ego. He is often depicted with four hands holding a book, a veena, an akshamala (crystal beads), and the chin-mudra, symbolizing worldly knowledge, the arts, yoga, and brahma vidya, respectively.

Dakshinamurti not only initiated the Guru Parampara but also manifests in the form of our gurus and guides us gently towards the supreme knowledge of the Self.

Sources: Suta Samhita, *Skanda Purana*

Fig. 6.1 Dakshinamurthi frieze, Meenakshi Temple, Madurai, Tamil Nadu

Source: Indiancorrector, Wikipedia

7

Nataraja

A peculiar rishi was worshiping a Shiva linga on the bank of a pond, amid a grove of milky Mangrove trees in Chidambaram, an ancient town in south India. His body was human, and his rudraksha and sacred ash marked him as a Shiva bhakta. But his eyes and legs were those of a tiger.

In time, another shocking muni arrived there. This new visitor had a human body with a snake's tail. Hearing the rustling of his arrival, the tiger-footed rishi stirred. He opened his large and sharp, tiger-like eyes. They gazed at each other for a few long seconds and smiled, divining that they were going to be eternal friends.

The tiger-legged rishi welcomed the visitor, "Oh Sage, your arrival has enlivened this sacred kshetram. I am the son of Rishi Madhyandina." Noticing the newcomer staring at him, he continued, "Let me assuage your curiosity about my eyes and legs. I wake up every morning, before sunrise, to climb the trees and pick fresh flowers to offer to our Lord Nataraja. The sap of the Thillai trees would often seep into my eyes, blurring my vision. My legs too were scarred with cuts and bruises. These physical discomforts were easy to ignore when faced with the immeasurable joy of worshiping the Lord. However, in his infinite compassion, Mahadeva blessed me with tiger eyes and legs to relieve my pain. Now, I am called Vyaghrapada, the tiger footed."

He paused for a breath and queried. "Who are you, Rishi? What brings you here?"

The snake-tailed visitor led Vyaghrapada to a rocky ledge, where they both sat. "It is my fortune to meet you, O Vyaghrapada. Mine is a long story. It was so long ago that I do not remember my origin or the time of my birth." He then went on to narrate the story of his origin.

Eons ago, the rishis of Darukavana and their wives stood transfixed, witnessing a wondrous scene. The skies too were getting crowded by devas, apsaras, and other celestial onlookers as Lord Shiva in the form of the strikingly handsome youth, Bhikshatana, danced the Ananda Tandava atop the Apasmara purusha (also called Muyalaka, the dwarf). The reason for this dance performance is a story for later. (See chapter on Bhikshatana.)

Back in Vaikunta, the snake Adi Shesha, who had borne Mahavishnu for eternity, felt the Lord becoming heavier. Surprised, he inquired about the reason. Mahavishnu replied, "I am watching the Ananda Tandava of Mahadeva through my divine vision. It fills me with such joy that I grow heavy."

Adi Shesha's curiosity was piqued. "I want to witness this dance, my Lord. Please allow me to be born as a human and visit Kailasha to watch it," he begged Mahavishnu. Mahavishnu assented to his faithful's desire.

Adi Shesha was born with a dimorphic body to the Saptarishi Atri and his wife Anusuya. They named him

Patanjali. When he came of age, he travelled to Kailasha in the hopes of witnessing the Lord's Ananda Tandavam. But Nandikeshwara stopped him at the gates, mocking Patanjali for his slimy, reptilian body.

That insult did not deter Patanjali. He instead composed a Nataraja stotram without any long vowels (dheerga sounds) that would use a "leg" or "horn" in Devanagari script (such as आ or की).

Anantamahasaṃ tridaśavandya charaṇaṃ muni hṛdantara vasantamamalam
kabandha viyadindvavani gandhavaha vahnimakha bandhuravimañju vapuṣam
anantavibhavaṃ trijagadantara maṇiṃ trinayanaṃ radhan khaṇḍana param
sananda muni vandita padaṃ sakaruṇaṃ para chidambara naṭaṃ hṛdi bhaja ॥ *5*

Worship with a full heart the great dancer, the Lord of Chidambaram.
His lustre is endless, and his feet are revered by the gods.
He is the pure one who resides in the hearts of sages.
His lovely body is made of water, sky, moon, earth, wind, fire, atman, and sun.
His glories are infinite; he is the jewel of the three worlds, having three eyes.
He smashed the three cities of Tripura.
The compassionate god who is saluted by Sage Sananda.
(*Nataraja Stotram*, verse 5, Patanjali)

Patanjali concluded his story. "Oh Vyaghrapada, as I prayed to Him outside the gates of Kailasha, Mahadeva spoke to my heart. He promised to dance the Ananda Tandavam for me in this Chidambara kshetram. That is why I am here."

Vyaghrapada trembled, his eyes raining tears. He said, "Rishi Patanjali, I have been yearning for years to watch his tandava. Please allow me to witness this vision with you."

Thus, at Patanjali's request, the Lord came to dance the Ananda Tandavam near the Thillai groves. It was witnessed by the ecstatic Vyaghrapada, Jaimini, and other rishis. Three thousand devout brahmanas, blessed by this vision, were tasked to manage the Chidambaram temple, a tradition that continues today.

The vision of this Tandava dance led to profound contributions to the world, through these rishis. Rishi Patanjali composed the Yoga Sutras based on the revelations from that darshan. Vyaghrapada wrote the *Chidambara Mahatmyam* capturing the essence of the Tandavam. Bharata Muni learnt the intricacies of dance from it and compiled the Natya Shastras, a treatise on dance. Rishi Panini crafted the Maheshwara Sutras, the foundational sounds of Sanskrit, from the Damaru of Shiva. Agastya Muni was inspired to lay the foundations of Tamil grammar.

Even today, scientists discover secrets of the universe in the form of Nataraja, the Lord of Dance.

Fritjof Capra, the scientist and author of the popular *The Tao of Physics*, writes: "The clearest image of the activity of God which any art or religion can boast of."

Carl Sagan, celebrated astrophysicist, says: "The dance that reveals the mysteries of the universe."

Lord Nataraja not only graces Indian temples but also dances at the entrance to CERN (European Organization for Nuclear Research), the world's largest particle accelerator in Switzerland, where the mysteries of the universe are studied.

Nataraja's dance is not merely an art form but the dance of creation and dissolution itself. The vibration of each atom, the slow sprouting of a plant, the blossoming and wilting of a flower, the foetus growing in the womb, the first breath of a baby, the stilling of one's breath, the gentle breeze, the violent storm, the winds that blow the desert sands, the crashing of waves, the gushing waterfalls, the clouds moving pregnant with rain, the planets spinning in space, the exploding stars, the black holes, the crashing of asteroids, every single movement is the dance of the universe.

Ananda Coomaraswamy, a renowned historian, says: "Every subatomic particle not only performs an energy dance but also is an energy dance; a pulsating process of creation and destruction, without end."

This profound symbolism is captured in this popular shloka, which is sung and danced to as a dhyana shloka in Bharatanatyam and other classical dance forms.

Aangikam bhuvanam yasya vachikam sarva vangmayam
aaharyam chandra taradi tam vande saattvikam shivam

The One whose body's movement is the entire Universe,

whose speech is all the languages of the world, and
whose ornaments are the moon and the stars,
To that pure Shiva, we bow.

Nataraja tattva appeals universally since each aspect of this form has spiritual, religious, creative, and scientific symbolism.

- Setting: The arch of flames, Prabha Mandalam, symbolizes the primal energy that manifests as creation. The lotus pedestal represents our mind and Apasmara, on whom Nataraja dances represents the ignorance about our true nature in our minds.
- Tresses: His flying tresses signify the continuous cycle of birth and death. Ganga, controlled in his tresses, symbolizes the life-giving energy for the regeneration of life.
- Arms: One hand holds the damaru, indicating the rhythm of the universe, which translates to days, seasons, tides, years, our bodies' circadian rhythms, and pralaya, the ultimate dissolution of the universe. Another hand holds Agni, which signifies the forces of creation and destruction. One lower hand shows the Abhaya mudra, inspiring fearlessness. The bent lower hand with its palm facing inward points at the raised left foot, diametrically opposite to the lower right arm. This symbolizes balance in creation.
- Legs: One foot is steadily dancing on Apasmara, while his other foot is lifted, indicating both order and chaos as part of creation. Devotees also consider the lifted foot, the *kunchitapadam*, as their refuge.

- Ornaments: He wears a short dhoti or tiger skin, the yagnopavitam (sacred thread), and two different earrings, signifying the duality of gender within him. The snake circling him represents the kundalini shakti manifest in us all.
- Face: His three eyes represent the sun, moon, and inner eye of knowledge. Further, Shiva smiles captivatingly, urging us to find joy despite the challenges of the world.

The two dances of Shiva, the Ananda "bliss" Tandavam and the Rudra "angry" Tandavam, represent creation and dissolution. A parallel dance by Shakti, the Lasya, is a sensual and graceful contrast to Shiva's Tandavam. Together, the dances symbolize all the stages of creation: *srshti* (creation), *sthiti* (preservation), *samharam* (dissolution), *tirodhana* (illusion), and *anugraha* (liberation).

While Lord Nataraja's dance pervades all of creation, Chidambaram, meaning "the sky of consciousness" remains the most popular kshetra where the Nataraja form is worshipped. It is one of the Pancha-bhuta Sthalas where Ishwara is worshipped as the akasha (sky element).

This magnificent temple with a golden roof laid by a Chola king houses three forms of Lord Shiva: the dynamic Nataraja, the approachable Akasha Linga, and an empty space called the Chidambara rahasya. Symbolically, a devotee begins by worshipping the dynamic form of Ishwara, graduates to perceiving the linga as *rupa-arupa*, both as form and formless, and finally realizes the Chidambara Rahasya, the formless nature of the Lord.

To the seeker, Nataraja's dance can be witnessed in the cosmic movements, the dynamism of nature, the seasons, the tides, to the changes in our own bodies.

Source: *Chidambara Mahatmyam*, Annaswamy Iyer

Fig. 7.1 Nataraja bronze in CERN, Geneva, Switzerland. Donated by Indian Government in 2004

8

Mrtyunjaya

Every parent rejoices at the sight of their children. However, when Rishi Mrkandu and his wife, Marudhvati, gazed at the radiant face of their young, brilliant son, Markandeya, their eyes drooped, and deep sorrow shrouded their countenance, escaping in deep sighs.

This anguish was the result of a choice they made years ago. They had prayed to Mahadeva for years, seeking a child. When Mahadeva finally heeded their call, he gave them a difficult choice.

"Mrkandu and Marudhvati, you have proven your bhakti with your diligent prayers. However, due to your past karmas, your child will be a cause for distress to you. You can choose to have a wise and good son who will live for sixteen short years, or you can have a dull and evil son with a long lifespan. Either way, you are destined to suffer. Choose now," said Shiva.

Mrkandu immediately picked the first option, sure that his wife would agree. Sixteen years seemed far away. The couple bowed down before the Lord, tears of gratitude streaming from their eyes.

Soon, a charming son was born to them. Markandeya, as they named him, grew up into a wise, courageous, and generous boy. He absorbed all the shastras from his teachers and grew to be noble of character. He naturally imbibed his parents' Shiva bhakti.

Despite their certainty of choice, as he grew older, so did their sorrow. They were helpless, unable to stop time. Yet, they kept the prophecy of Markandeya's impending death from him. They worried that the knowledge of his destiny would scare him. They pretended to be happy.

However, Markandeya sensed their growing fear. As he turned fifteen, a year away from his death, his parents' anxiety for his life could no longer be concealed.

Markandeya confronted them. "Mata, pita, while other parents celebrate their children's birthdays with pujas and yagnas, you ignore mine. Despite your love for me, you rarely smile at me these days. Have I done something to upset you? Please tell me."

Marudhvati broke down in uncontrollable sobs. The truth could no longer be hidden from their son. Mrkandu narrated the story of Markandeya's birth to him.

"Markandeya, we are blessed to have you as our son. You have brought us immense joy. Yet a fatal destiny awaits you. Due to our Karma, we must suffer your death. The day was prophesized to be your sixteenth birthday." Mrkandu sighed as he explained.

To Markandeya's credit, he did not succumb to despair. The rare emotion of bhakti had sprouted in his young heart. Shiva, his ishta deva, seemed to inspire him with a plan.

He addressed his parents, comforting them. "Mata, Pita, I am blessed to be your son. You have instilled in me this bhakti I feel toward Sadashiva. I believe he can aid me in my plight. I will dedicate this year of my life to him. I will visit sacred kshetras, bathe in holy rivers, fast, and chant the Panchakshari every waking moment. After that, I will accept his will. Please bless me."

Receiving his parents' tearful blessings, he embarked on a teertha yatra, a long pilgrimage. He walked across Bharatavarsha, from Kailasha to Kanyakumari, his thoughts immersed in Mahadeva.

Finally, as his sixteenth birthday approached, he ended up in the lovely temple of Amritaghateswara in contemporary Thirukkadaiyur, Tamil Nadu. This kshetra had an ancient legend associated with it.

Kalpas ago, when the devas and asuras assembled to partake of the divine nectar that emerged from the churning of the milky ocean, Ganesha was miffed. "The devas and asuras did not worship me before they started the churning. They need a reminder," he explained to his mushika. He purloined the amrita-ghata, the pot of nectar, and ran to this kshetra.

Arriving there, pot in hand, Ganesha pondered what to do with it. "My father, Mahadeva, imbibed the kalakuta poison that emerged during the churning, thereby protecting the world from being burned. Yet, he did not receive any part of the riches from the ocean. So, the first drop of the *amrita* is rightfully his."

He crafted a linga and poured a handful of amrita on it before handing it back to the devas. This linga came to be called Amrtaghateshwara, the bestower of immortality upon its worshippers.

Therefore, it was divine providence that brought Markandeya to this kshetra on his birthday, prophesied to be his last day. He knew that Yama Dharmaraja, the God of Death, was punctual at collecting jeevas. Markandeya immersed himself in tapas by chanting the special Mahamrtyunjaya mantra.

Oṃ tryámbakaṃ yajāmahe sugandhíṃ puṣṭi-vardhánam
urvārukam íva bandhánān mṛtyor mukṣīya mā'mṛtā́t

I worship that fragrant, three-eyed One who nourishes all living entities.
Like the fruit falling off from the bondage of the stem,
May we be liberated from death and mortality.
(*Rigveda* 7.59.12, attributed to Vasiṣṭha)

Markandeya sensed a sudden disturbance. Through his siddhis, he could hear the clatter of Yamaraja and his ganas, a sound beyond human perception. The ganas were cheering for young blood while the dignified Yama entered the sanctum holding his pasha, the noose, ready to fling on Markandeya.

Markandeya had surrendered to Mahadeva. With his arms around the linga, he clung to it, as Yama's pasha tightened around him. The pasha could not avoid the linga, as Markandaya had wrapped himself around it. What a sacrilege! Yama had inadvertently attempted to entrap the Mahakala himself.

Mahakala emerged from the linga, blazing with rage, and kicked Yama. The God of Death met his own end. However, Death was necessary for maintaining balance in the universe.

As Markandeya cried with gratitude, Bhumi Devi, Mother Earth, cried in sorrow. "O Prabhu, the world needs Yamaraja. Please forgive him for his mistake. He was merely executing Markandeya's fate. Can destiny be changed?"

"I did prophesize Markandeya's death at sixteen," Shiva agreed. He continued, "There is a way out. Markandeya will remain immortal, never to age beyond sixteen. He will continue to live across many kalpas."

Shiva then revived Yama and earned the name, Kala Samhara Murti, the slayer of Yama. He blesses all who worship him at this kshetra with longevity.

Today, the kshetra of Amrtaghateshwara, Mrtyunjaya, or Kala Samhara Murti is popular for performing shastiabdhapurthi (60th birthday) or sathabhishekam (80th birthday) for those seeking a long life.

Invoking Mrytyunjaya, one can banish their fear of mortality, through the realization that we are the immortal Atman.

Source: *Tirukkadaiyur Sthala Puranam*

Fig. 8.1 Markandeya clings on to Shiva Linga as Yama approaches. Painting by Raja Ravi Varma

9

Kirata

Arjuna, the famed Pandava warrior, sat before a linga he had shaped from sand, on the beautiful slopes of the Indrakhila hills, near contemporary Vijayawada in Andhra Pradesh. He was immersed in deep tapas, seeking the Pashupatastra, the greatest of weapons.

Arjuna, an expert archer and a methodical warrior, believed in preparation and discipline. He was utilizing the Pandavas' thirteen years of exile to acquire special weapons for the great war looming in the inevitable future. His intense tapas caused his body to radiate heat like a forest fire. It started scorching the Indrakhila forests. Animals screeched, and swarms of birds flew out to escape a horrible death. The helpless residents of the hill beseeched the sages to protect them. The rishis sought Shiva, requesting him to intervene.

Oblivious to these events, Arjuna continued his tapas, his senses trained on Mahadeva.

He sensed a sudden intrusion in his surroundings. A nasty guttural roar came from nearby. Opening his eyes, Arjuna saw a fierce boar, panting in rage, saliva dripping from its mouth, with its bloodshot eyes trained on him. It was ready to attack. As it leaped, the agile Arjuna picked up his bow, in a flash, rolled over onto his back, and shot an arrow into the bore's chest, a moment before it landed on him. It screeched loudly as his powerful arrow ripped through its corpulent flesh. Or so Arjuna thought as he stood up and dusted his clothes.

He looked up as he heard humans approaching. A small procession of kiratas, local hunters, were coming his way, headed by a young, boorish hunter and a huntress. A motley gang of hunters was running behind them, while beating their drums and yelling slogans.

"O my dear husband, you shot the massive boar," sang the lady, dressed in beads and wildflowers, as the group approached the dead boar.

Arjuna's ego was hurt. The renowned warrior who had single-handedly won wars against great armies wanted credit for bringing down a mere boar.

Miffed, he waved off her claims, saying, "Oh, Lady, don't make up stories to please your husband. I shot that boar. See, that is my arrow." As he pointed at the boar, he noticed another arrow beside his. Both arrows had struck the bore at the exact same place on its chest. Noticing the same thing, the hunter and his wife sniggered.

Arjuna was enraged. "You savages dare to mock me? Don't you know who I am? The whole world knows me as the greatest archer. Haven't you heard of me, Arjuna?" He was about to leave when the hunter stopped him.

"Arjuna? I don't know anybody by that name. If you think you are so great, let's have a battle. Let's see who wins." The hunter lifted his rustic bow and notched an arrow.

Arjuna couldn't suppress his laughter. "You want me to fight with you, a lowly Kirata? I will decimate you with one arrow and return to my Shiva worship." He lifted his Gandiva and shot his first arrow at the hunter, expecting this skirmish to be over before it began.

Hours later, the battle continued. Arjuna had deployed his most powerful *astras*, and his arrow case was depleted. In disbelief, he pulled out his sword to duel with the hunter. Soon that too was flicked off into the air. Shocked, Arjuna hesitated. A true warrior doesn't rely on weapons. He started wrestling with the hunter. After a short tussle, the hunter lifted Arjuna up and effortlessly hurled him to the ground.

At the hunter's touch, a strange thrill spread through Arjuna. "Who is this hunter? He cannot be an ordinary kirata," he wondered. "Is it Karna in disguise to kill me? Is it my father, Indra, teaching me a lesson? Is it Krishna playing a prank on me? Or is it... is it the one I have been praying to?" He rose from the ground and looked straight at the hunter as realization dawned on him. "Oh Lord, it is you!"

The kirata and his wife erupted in mirthful laughter. "Yes, Arjuna. It is me. And Devi here. I am pleased by your tapas. The Pashupatrastra that you seek is too powerful to be given to unworthy people. So, I wanted to test your mettle myself. For you to be at war with me for so many hours proves that you are worthy." The Lord blessed Arjuna and proceeded to instruct him on the correct usage of the weapon.

Arjuna fell to the feet of the divine couple and revelled in the magnanimity of the Lord and the compassion of Devi Parvati, who both took a humble disguise to bless him.

Naturally, sculptors have been inspired by this mesmerizing incident. Arjuna's penance has been immortalized in the famed Mamallapuram temple, and Bhagavan, as Kirata, appears in many temples holding the arrow and bow. The great poet Bharavi took this simple episode and blew it up into eighteen cantos of beautiful verses as Kiratarjuniyam, one of the Mahakavyas of Sanskrit.

One of the most touching mentions of the Adi Kirata is by Bhagawan Adi Shankaracharya, who invites Shiva as the Kirata, the hunter, to kill the dark wild animals that reside in our own minds.

Mā gaccha tvamitastatō giriśabhō mayyēva vāsaṁ kuru
svāmin ādikirāta māmaka manaḥ kāntārasīmantarē
vartantē bahuśōmr̥gāmadajuṣō mātsaryamōhādayastān
hatvā mr̥gayā vinōdarucitā lābhaṁ ca samprāpsyasi

Oh Girisha, do not go here and there; reside only within me.
Oh Swami, Oh primeval hunter!
Within the boundaries of the dark forest of my mind,
There are many rutting animals, like jealousy, delusion, etc.
Having killed them, you will enjoy the hunt,
while clearing my mind of the wild animals.
(*Shivanandalahari*, verse 43, Adi Shankaracharya)

The beautiful allegory compares our mind to a dark forest (kantara) and the agitations and turbulence of our minds to the wild beasts that live there. These animals embodying lust, anger, greed, delusion, pride, and envy (kama, krodha, lobha, moha, mada, and matsarya) run rampant in our minds. Knowledge and self-control cannot keep them permanently tamed.

May the Adi Kirata reside in our minds and hunt the wild animals that roam in it.

Source: Vana and Kairata Parvas, Mahabharata

Fig. 9.1 Shiva as Kirata with Parvati as a huntress and Arjuna in penance. The boar killed by both is seen below. Sculpture on the Gopuram of the Kapaleeshwara temple, Chennai

Source: https://stonestoriessite.wordpress.com

10

Bhikshatana

Mahadeva established himself as the greatest thespian in the universe in another exciting appearance. This wondrous drama unfolded in Darukavana, a forest in contemporary Gujarat.

A large group of rishis had established their ashramas there. They led a religious life with their wives, children, and disciples. However, they believed that performing yagnas, rituals and sacrifices would lead to moksha. These rishis completely disregarded the need for devotion towards Bhagawan (bhakti yoga) or the importance of the knowledge of the Upanishads (*jnana* yoga). (This darshana, a school of thought, is called Purva Mimamsa.) Over time, they had gained many siddhis, yogic powers, through such rituals. This gave birth to pride.

Mahadeva, being the jagat guru—the teacher of the universe—takes his role of guiding confused jeevas quite seriously. In his compassion, he takes the form most befitting the lesson that the student needs to learn, like his form of the youthful, silent, and celibate Dakshinamurti to appeal to the mature Santkumaras. (See chapter on Dakshinamurti.)

For the rishis of Darukavana, he chose the form of Bhikshatana, a naked mendicant. He brought along with him Mohini, the alluring feminine form of Mahavishnu.

One lovely spring evening in that verdant forest, the rishis' wives were solemnly preparing the offerings for the yagnas. From the woods, an enchanting, naked youth wandered into the clearing, shaking his hips, with provocative glances at the women. Taken aback by this vision, the rishi-patnis froze mid-task and gaped at this newcomer. Their minds, disciplined by a life of austerity, started to race. Improper thoughts filled their minds. "Who is this handsome man? How will it feel to touch him, to be embraced by his perfect body?"

The youth sauntered around them, winking at them, and making lewd gestures. As they fell into his seductive spell, he re-entered the woods, beckoning them. The rishi-patnis followed him like puppets pulled on a string. All their chores were left behind. Milk boiled over. Flowers gathered to thread garlands scattered in the breeze. Birds flew in to peck on the half-prepared food. The cows waiting to be milked, mooed.

Soon the rishis noticed the disappearance of their wives. Perplexed, they followed their trail into the woods only to find their pativrata wives in the erotic thrall of the young Bhikshatana. Rage overpowered them. Some rishis ordered their wives back, cursing them for their debauchery, while others tried to drag their women violently.

Before they could act on their rage, another enchanting vision appeared before their eyes. Mohini materialized near the rishis, sashaying seductively, and fluttering her eyelashes at them. The rishis were enamoured by her allure. "What grace. Such seductive curves of her bosom and hips. If only I could make her mine." Lecherous thoughts flooded their minds as she teased them, playing with her garment. As she glided into the woods, they followed her, their anger and yagnas forgotten.

One of the rishis snapped out of that lustful daze. "Stop, brothers. We have fallen under this woman's spell. And our virtuous wives must have been bewitched by that youth. It is a trick to prevent us from performing our yagnas and acquiring more power."

This realization jolted the rishis awake. They marched to destroy the prankster, Bhikshatana.

Using their siddhis, the rishis hurled a mad deer at the lad. Smiling, the youth caught the deer like a toy and tossed it to the ground, where it lay whimpering. They conjured a venomous snake and flung it at him. The youth caught it and wrapped it around his neck. The snake hissed but settled calmly, encircling his neck. The rishis conjured a man-eating tiger that charged at the youth, baring its sharp teeth. The youth captured it by its neck and ripped open its jaws with his bare hands. He choked the tiger to death. Then, skinning it in an instant, he wore the pelt across his torso, like a shawl.

Astonished, the rishis summoned a wild elephant to trample the youth. In seconds, he grabbed the elephant's trunk in a viselike grip and flung it by its trunk onto the ground, killing it. He skinned it and wrapped the pelt around his hips as a dhoti.

The rishis should have realized that this was no ordinary lecherous youth. But their ego wouldn't let them concede.

They combined their potent siddhis and produced a dwarfish asura called Apasmara (or Muyalakan). The asura screeched in an abrasive voice as he leaped at Bhikshatana. As the rishis watched intently, there was a dizzying play of arms and legs. Apasmara landed on the ground, face in the dirt. Roaring in glee, Bhikshatana climbed on Apasmara's back and started dancing, his legs rising in agile motions, his fingers forming intricate mudhras, and his expressive face displaying the navarasas, the nine emotions.

Mohini clapped her hands in rhythm. From the skies came the musical accompaniments from the veena, mrdangam and cymbals. The invisible devas, gandharvas, and kinnaras cheered, mesmerized. They showered flowers over this master dancer.

Each step of Bhikshatana's dance dismantled the egos of the rishis. They realized that the youth they had dared to fight was none other than Mahadeva.

They prostrated before him and begged for pardon. "O Lord, we were blinded by our egos. You have shattered it. But what brings you down here in this strange avatar? Why this lila, Prabho?" they asked.

Bhikshatana then transformed into Dakshinamurthi, the great guru and taught them true knowledge. "While yagnas can give you worldly treasures, special siddhis, and attainment of the heavens, they cannot lead you to moksha. Ishwara grants the fruits of yagnas, so you must cultivate bhakti. You must also seek the knowledge of the Upanishads to realize the Atman. That is the only way to moksha. I came to teach you this lesson."

This was not the only time the Lord took the form of Bhikshatana.

Once, proud of his creative power, Brahma developed an ego and lied to win a contest against Mahavishnu. To punish him for this violation of truth, Shiva beheaded one of the five heads of Brahma. And thus, Brahma was left with four heads. (Refer to the story on Arunachala.)

As Mahadeva submits to the dharma he instituted in the universe, he atoned for cutting off Brahma's head by taking the form of a humble beggar, Bhikshatana, and wandered around with the kapala (skull) seeking alms or bhiksha. A sweet detail to this legend is that he also accepted bhiksha from Devi Annapurna in Kashi.

Interestingly, while the story of Bhikshatana seems to have originated in Gujarat or Kashi, this form is popular in Karnataka, Tamil Nadu, and Odisha, with beautiful iconography in many temples. Often, he is depicted like Bhairava, accompanied by a dog. His murti is often surrounded by those of lustful rishi-patnis and angry rishis.

A 7th-century Shaiva saint, Appar, sang a ninda stuti, a praise that appears insulting, about the handsome Bhikshatana, seducer of married women. He spoke of women allured by Bhikshatana's appearance, speech, and glance. Mahadeva warned these women of his deceptions, yet they could not stop themselves from falling for him.

vaNNaN^kaL thAmpATi van^thu n^inRu
valicheythu vaLaikavarn^thAr vakaiyAl n^ammaik
kaNNampAl n^inReythu kanalap pEchik
kaTiyathOr viTaiyERik kApA liyAr
chuNNaN^kaL rad^koNTu thuthaiyap pUchith
thOluTuththu n^UlpUNTu thOnRath thOnRa
aNNalAr pOkinRAr van^thu kANIr
azakiyarE AmAththUr aiya nArE.
Ven^thArveN poTippUchi veLLai mAlai
virichaTaimER RanychUTi vINai yEn^thik
kan^thAran^ thAmuralAp pOkA n^iRkak

Singing songs, He came, and forcing me.
He snatched my bangles.
Casting dart-like looks on us,
He made us give in.
His burning words stirred our passion.
Bedaubed with gold-dust, clad in skin,
And adorned with the white thread,
Kaapali, the noble One, the handsome One.
The Lord of Aamaatthoor moves away.
Come and behold Him!
(Thevaram—6th Tirumurai, 6.9.1, Tirunavukkarasar)

Bhikshatana can also enchant us, free us from desires, and lead us to Him.

Source: Shatarudra Samhita, *Shiva Purana*

Fig. 10.1 Bhikshatana at Kailashanatha Temple, Kanchipuram, Pallava period (7th century CE) sculpture. Naked youth followed by rishi-patnis. The rishi (*top left*) is angry and about to hit Bhikshatana
Source: http://picasaweb.google.com/injamaven

11

Sharabeshwara

The rakshasa Hiranyakashipu was a fanatical egomaniac. He mandated that he be worshipped and forbade the worship of Hari. His subjects did not dare disobey him, but someone in his own family did. His son Prahlada had discovered Hari bhakti when he was in his mother's womb, listening in utero to Narada Muni's stories of Lord Mahavishnu.

Hiranyakashipu appointed two able teachers, Sanda and Amarka, to rid Prahlada of his Hari bhakti. Instead, Prahlada ended up turning the other students into Hari bhaktas.

Enraged by his failure to mould his own son, he threatened, punished, and tortured Prahlada in horrific ways. Prahlada was fed poison, toppled from the mountain, and even immolated. But he survived all the ordeals unscathed. His face retained its tranquil smile despite such trials.

This served to heighten Hiranyakashipu's rage. Dragging Prahlada into his hall, he thundered, "Where is this Hari you venerate? Is he in this room? Is he within this pillar?"

Prahlada's knowledge of Vishnu was firm. "Yes, father. He is everywhere, even in you and me. And of course, in that pillar too." He smiled. Hiranyakashipu thought his son was taunting him. He smashed the pillar with his mace.

As the pillar crumbled, a terrifying vision appeared from within the dust. A startling creature with the head and claws of a lion and the torso and legs of a human walked out of the pillar. The mighty Hiranyakashipu stepped back, panicked. This was Narasimha, an avatara of Mahavishnu. He pounced on Hiranyakashipu and ripped him apart with his claws that evening at the threshold of the palace. The entire kingdom was relieved. They were liberated from the rakshasa at last.

However, Narasimha's wrath did not dissipate with the death of Hiranyakashipu. His chest heaved, he growled, and the hairs on his red mane stood up on their ends, like a halo of sharp swords.

His fury was so terrifying that even his consort, Lakshmi, kept away from him. The devas prayed to Shiva for deliverance. They knew of Shiva and Vishnu's mutual love and respect and their history of coming to the aid of the other in times of need.

Shiva, appearing as Veerabhadra, attempting to pacify Narasimha with wise counsel. He said, "O Narasimha, your task is complete. Discard this form and return to your *shanta rupam*, your benign form." The advice had no impact on Narasimha. He continued to prance, growling, and gesticulating, with his fangs dripping saliva. Shiva then resorted to threats. But that did not mollify him either. Narasimha had entered a state of rage, from which only another's fury could draw him out.

A startling lila ensued. Mahadeva transformed into a more fearsome creature called Sharaba, combining bird, lion, and human in one incredulous form. Sharaba appeared as a golden bird, with the torso of a human, two red enticing eyes, four hunched lion legs touching the ground with claws unsheathed, four legs with claws upward and an animal tail swishing behind him. He hovered above on two massive wings, infused with the powers of goddesses Durga and Pratyangira.

Sharaba then goaded Narasimha into a duel. The battle between the two fierce manifestations of Hara and Hari continued. They ran across the world, chasing each other. When Sharabeshwara took to the skies, Narasimha followed in the form of a two-headed bird called Gandaberunda. Pratyangira fought with Gandaberunda until they all crashed to earth. They could sense that Narasimha's temper had lessened.

Sharaba tentatively hugged Narasimha, muttering calming words into his ear till the latter's rage subsided. His breath steadied, his eyes closed, and his mane fell upon his still shoulders. He assumed the form of Yoga Narasimha. Relieved, Lakshmi sat on his lap and held him. In this form, he blessed Prahlada.

This dynamic story is a touching display of the bond between Shiva and Vishnu.

Vishnu also returned the favour when Shiva's generosity got him into trouble.

An asura once engaged in tapas to gain Shiva's favour. When Shiva appeared before him, he requested a strange boon. "The person's head I place my hand on will burn to ashes. Please grant me this boon, O Mahadeva." The benevolent Shiva consented.

The crooked Bhasmasura decided to try the boon on the giver. He was certain that the boon of the mighty Mahadeva would act on all, including him. The asura chased Shiva through the woods. Vishnu intervened in this embarrassing situation.

He arrived in the woods in the form of the seductive Mohini. The chase forgotten, the asura ogled at her beauty. Fluttering her eyelashes, she beckoned him closer with an inviting smile. As he was about to embrace her, she started dancing to a bewitching tune. Her feet and hips moved languorously while she tossed her silky hair and scorched him with tempting glances. Bhasmasura fell under her spell and started mimicking her dance.

As Shiva watched this drama unfold, Mohini's arms formed the lotus mudhra and Bhasmasura imitated her. The dance picked up pace, the feet and gestures grew more frantic and complex. Casually, Mohini placed her hand on her well-coiffed tresses, and Bhasmasura unthinkingly, followed suit. He laid his palm on his own tangled mass of hair and Mahadeva's boon took immediate effect. Bhasmasura was reduced to ashes in the blink of an eye.

These enchanting stories of Shiva and Vishnu not only reveal their friendship and mutual admiration but also lead us to the realization of their oneness.

Source: Shatarudra Samhita, *Shiva Purana*

12

Hari-Hara

Who is greater? Vishnu or Shiva? This is a common, yet futile question born of ignorance.

rudrasya paramo viṣṇur viṣṇoścaparamaḥ śivaḥ ||
eka eva dvidhā bhūto
loke carati nityaśaḥ ||

Shiva is the Lord of Vishnu, and Vishnu is the Lord of Shiva.
The One Lord is moving around the world in two forms!
(*Hari Vamsa*, verse 37.65–37.66)

Reflecting the great rishis, commoners in the society also mocked those who considered Hari and Siva as separate, competing entities.

hariyum sivanum onnu,
ariyadhavar vaayila mannu

Hari and Shiva are one.
Stuff with mud the mouth of the one
who doesn't accept this.
(Tamil folk quote)

The two lords reveal their unity through diverse expressions. Sometimes, they stand as friends helping each other. In other instances, they are each other's greatest devotees. Nevertheless, their essence radiates in their Oneness.

Vishnu as Shiva Bhakta

During an ancient kalpa, asura sons of Diti, the daityas, wreaked havoc across the universe, disrupting sacred rituals and agricultural activities. The devas, unable to fend off the numerous and vicious asuras armies, sought Vishnu's protection.

They lamented, "Lord, our weapons have no effect on these asuras. As though they are immortal, they rise again and procreate huge hordes. Please help us!"

Vishnu assented, for it was his responsibility to protect the innocent. Recognising the urgency and need of the hour, he sought something more powerful to control this menace.

He went to Kailasha and worshipped Mahadeva for a long time. However, Adideva was in intense tapas and did not awaken. Undeterred, Vishnu recited the Shiva Sahasranama—the thousand special names of Shiva—and offered a blue lotus for each name. Through Shiva's divine lila, the thousandth blue lotus went missing. When all his search failed, Vishnu decided to scoop out his own eye and offer it instead, as his eyes are compared to the lotus: *aravinda lochana*, *kamala nayana*, and *rajiva netra.*

Touched, Shiva offered to give any boon to Mahavishnu.

"O Mahadeva, all the weapons we have are ineffective against the vast army of daityas. Please bless me with a weapon that can wipe them out instantly," he beseeched.

Mahakala bestowed the Sudarshana Chakra upon him. It shone like a thousand suns, was as fast as thought, and could scorch through large armies in an instant. The Sudarshana Chakra became Mahavishnu's preferred weapon in many battles and fights to uphold the good.

Mahavishnu expressed his Shiva bhakti through his avataras.

Rama worshiped Rameshwara after the war with Ravana to atone for killing brahmanas. (See the chapter on Rameshwara.)

Krishna sought Mahadeva's blessings for a son. All the ashta mahishis, or the eight wives of Sri Krishna, except Jambavati, had given birth to several children. She urged Krishna to pray for a son for her. Krishna foresaw the end of Yadu dynasty at the hands of his son born to Jambavati. Yet, he could not deny her.

Under Upamanyu Muni's guidance, he performed the difficult Pashupata vrata in the Prabhasa kshetram. Pleased, Mahadeva appeared with Gauri and blessed him to beget a son by Jambavati.

Soon after, Jambavati delivered a boy. Sri Krishna named him Samba (Sa-Amba) to acknowledge him as the blessing of Shiva with Amba. He shone as a great warrior in the Mahabharata War. But his prank on a rishi led to the destruction of Yadavas.

Shiva as Vishnu Bhakta

Shiva revels in Rama Bhakti as well.

He gives upadesha to Parvathi in this famous shloka of the Vishnu Sahasranama where he states that the holy name of Rama is equal to the thousand names of Vishnu.

sri rama rama rameti rame rame manorame |
sahasra-naama tat-tulyam rama-naama varaanane ||

Dear Parvati, by meditating "Rama Rama Rama",
My mind gets absorbed in Rama.
Rama Nama is equal to the thousand names of God.
(*Vishnu Sahasranama Stotram*, Uttara Bhaga)

In two retellings of the Ramayana, the Adhyatma Ramayana in the *Brahmanda Purana* and the Ramacharita Manasa, Shiva narrates the extraordinary story of Rama to Parvati.

Shankara Narayana

While the stories depict them as two separate gods, they emphatically demonstrated their oneness as Shankara Narayana.

Devotees of Shiva and Vishnu once quarrelled over whose god was bigger. Their immaturity moved Parvati to request Shiva and Vishnu to resolve this issue collaboratively. They appeared as Hari-Hara or Shankara Narayana, or half Shiva and half Vishnu to exemplify their oneness. This form, evident in cave paintings from the 5th century, signifies the concept of unity in duality. This form has popped up in cave temples, like Badami. Several temples in Karnataka, Tamil Nadu, and Kerala are dedicated to this form.

Shiva and Vishnu emphasize their unity, echoed by Sri Krishna in Mahabharata. He teaches Arjuna in the Shanti Parva, "He who knows Rudra knows me, and he who knows me knows Rudra. He who follows Rudra follows me; Rudra is Narayana. Both are one, manifest in two forms."

śaivaṃ ca vaiṣṇavaṃ rūpamekarūpaṃ narottama
dvayośca aṃtaraṃ nāsti ekarūpamahātmanoḥ |
śivāya viṣṇurūpāya śivarūpāya viṣṇave
śivasya hṛdayaṃ viṣṇurviṣṇośca hṛdayaṃ śivaḥ |

O king, the form of Shiva and that of Vishnu are identical.
There is no difference between the glorious two, who are of the same form.
Salute Shiva in the form of Vishnu, and
Vishnu in the form of Śiva.
Vishnu is the heart of Shiva, and Shiva is the heart of Vishnu.
(*Padma Purana*, verse 2.71.19–2.71.20)

One must seek the knowledge of the oneness of Hari-Hara that pervades the universe.

Sources: Sudarshana Chakra, Kotirudra Samhita (*Shiva Purana*); Hari Vamsha Parva 3.84.11 (Mahabharata); and Birth of Samba, Vayaveeya Samhita (*Shiva Purana*)

Fig 12.1 Hari-Hara, Shiva and Vishnu in one combined form, in Harihar, a 12th-century Hoysala temple, Karnataka

13

Neelakantha

Devatas in the Sanatana dharma pantheon portray a spectrum of skin colours: black Krishna and Kali, bluish-hued Vishnu, greenish Devi, golden Lakshmi, smoky Ganesha, and the dazzling white Mahadeva.

However, Bhagavan is the creator and storehouse of all colours. The great Shiva bhakta Rishi Upamanyu describes Shiva in the Mahabharata as one with many colours.

gaurah śyāmastathā kṛṣṇah
pāṇduro dhūmalohitah ।

He is fair, he is darkish, he is dark, he is pale, he is of the colour of smoke, and he is red.
(Anusasanika Parva, chapter 14, Mahabharata)

However, for the purposes of meditation, he is generally considered white-complexioned and enveloped or surrounded by white.

gātraṃ bhasmasitaṃ sitaṃ cha hasitaṃ hastē kapālaṃ sitaṃ
khaṭvāṅgaṃ cha sitaṃ sitaścha vṛṣabhaḥ karṇē sitē kuṇḍalē ।
gaṅgā phēnasitā jaṭā paśupatēśchandraḥ sitō mūrdhani
sō'yaṃ sarvasitō dadātu vibhavaṃ pāpakṣayaṃ sarvadā ॥

May the white Deva grant that power that always destroys sins!
White is his body, covered with ashes.
White are his laughing teeth, the skull, and the club he holds.
White is his bull, his earrings, and the foamy Ganges,
White is his matted hair and the Moon on His head.
(*Shiva Aparadha Kshamapana Stotram*, verse 17, Adi Shankaracharya)

Yet, the color that is most associated with him is blue, as he is often called Neelakantha, one with the blue neck. The story behind this is well known, yet it gets more fascinating with successive retellings.

In the Shweta Varaha Kalpa, during the churning of the ksheera sagara or the milky ocean, the devas and asuras agreed to collaborate. Both sides wanted to obtain the divine nectar that promised immortality. They believed that they could handle this monumental task by themselves. However, they soon discovered that for the churning to succeed, they would need the timely help of Mahavishnu and Mahadeva.

With the commencement of the churning, the Mandara mountain, used as the churning rod, started to sink into the ocean. Mahavishnu became Kurma, a tortoise, to support the sinking mountain, leading the devas and asuras to believe that they were doing the hard work.

With the immense power of the Kurma avatara, the waters of the ocean started swirling, creating huge waves. Churning the snake rope, the devas and asuras eagerly awaited treasures to emerge from the ocean. Instead, they started gagging over pungent fumes arising from the ocean. What started as a mild odour soon became a toxic miasma, hanging like a cloud over the entire ocean.

"Oh, these terrible fumes. Is it from the ocean or from Vasuki's mouth?" They looked around helplessly for its source, even as their eyes burned. They covered their faces with their upper clothes, but to no avail. "Oh, it's burning me. Help! I cannot see." they cried. In seconds, the lethal poison started eating away at their insides. They cried to Mahavishnu again for help. Vishnu informed them that the Kalakuta poison had emerged due to the churning of the ocean and that it could wipe out every living thing in the universe. Only Mahadeva could help in this situation.

Desperate, the devas invoked Sadashiva. "Pashupati, protector of all creatures, you are our one hope in the face of this calamity."

Mahavishnu chimed in with a teasing smile. "Rudra, you are the foremost among gods. Hence, it is only fitting that you take the first things to emerge from the ocean. Please partake of this Kalakuta poison as your sacrificial oblation, your ahuti."

Sadashiva roared with laughter at this openly opportunistic explanation. Yet, to save all of creation, Sadashiva suctioned the fast-spreading, black-hued kalakuta into his palm and gulped it down like it was ambrosia.

Adi Shankaracharya enchantingly questions Bhagavan about this lila.

jvālōgraḥ sakalāmarāti-bhayadaḥ kśvēlaḥ kathaṃ vā tvayā
dṛśṭaḥ kiṃ cha karē dhṛtaḥ kara-talē kiṃ pakva-jambū-phalam
jihvāyāṃ nihitaścha siddha-ghuṭikā vā kaṇṭha-dēśē bhṛtaḥ
kiṃ tē nīla-maṇir-vibhūśaṇam-ayaṃ śambhō mahātman vada

How did you perceive the fiery poison,
which terrified even the devas?
When you carried it in your hand,
did it appear like a ripe plum to you?
When you placed it on your tongue,
did it feel like medicinal pills from the doctor?
When it went down your throat,
did it appear like a blue gem to you?
Hey, Shambho, please tell us.
(*Shivananda Lahari*, verse 32, Adi Shankaracharya)

Parvati's hand shot out to squeeze his neck, in a panicked attempt to prevent the poison from going down his throat to his stomach. Perhaps, as Jaganmatha, the universal mother, she wished to protect the creation that was housed in his stomach. Her divine touch may have converted the kalakuta, poison, into ksheera or milk.

That poison lent a dazzling blue hue to his white neck, giving birth to the new moniker Neelakantha or the blue-necked one.

Subsequently, the devas and asuras went back to churn the ocean. Many divine beings and treasures arose from the ocean. The divine beings Mahalakshmi, the apsaras, and Varuna; the divine animals Kamadenu, Airavata, and Ucchaishravas; the divine treasures Kaustubha, Kalpavrksha, and Sharanga, etc., manifested from the depths of the ksheera sagar. The devas claimed most of these riches. Mahalakshmi chose Vishnu, who was also offered the Kaustubha and the Sharanga bow.

Shiva regarded these treasures with complete indifference. He, after all, is the epitome of dispassion. However, when the moon, Chandra, emerged, it was offered to him to cool the heat of the Kalakuta. With a sublime smile, Mahadeva placed Chandra on his forehead, thereby earning for himself the names Somashekhara and Chandramouli.

Mahatmas equate Samudra Manthan, the churning of the ocean, to the sadhana and contemplation that sadhakas and yogis undertake in their minds. Often, the first to appear are toxic emotions from our subconscious, built over many lifetimes. Offering them to Neelakantha initiates the process of purifying the mind.

Sources: Vasudeva Mahatmya, Vaishnava Khanda (*Skanda Purana*); Adi Parva (Mahabharata); and Rudra Samhita, Sati Khanda (*Shiva Purana*)

14

Matrbhuteshwara

The Brahmapuram temple was busier than usual for it was the harvest season. All the farming families prayed for a bountiful harvest and devotees washed their feet or bathed in the temple tank. Brahmanas offered *arghya* (water) to Surya Bhagavan as they did their morning ablutions.

A few feet away from the temple tank, a toddler sat sobbing in distress. His cries went unheard by the crowd. Forsaken and alone, he looked around for his parents, whimpering pitiably.

His mother would have immediately responded to the child's hunger and fed him. All prayers and rituals would have taken a backseat to her child's needs. However, his devout father, Shivapada Hrdayar, who had brought the baby along with him, was absorbed in his prayers. He was oblivious to his child's cries.

Unable to locate his father, the child looked up at the gopuram, the temple tower, on the other side of the temple tank. His eyes fell upon the sculpture of a majestic couple seated on a bull. To the distressed child, they oozed *vatsalyam*, parental compassion. Eyes fixed on them, his cries grew louder.

In a flash, the sculptures transformed. Radiating light, they came alive. An alluring man and a beautiful woman sat on a white bull. The graceful lady descended from the bull with a golden bowl. She picked him up and held him in her lap. From the bowl, she fed him some sweet milk. He gulped it down, ravenous. When he was sated, she placed him down gently, sat back on the bull beside that regal man, and disappeared.

Meanwhile, in the temple tank, his father, realizing the time, ran to check on his son. He noticed some milk dribbling down his chin and assumed that some stranger had fed his child. Unable to locate the person, he directed his anger towards the innocent child.

"How dare you accept food from strangers?" He roared, "Who fed you?" The child was eerily calm. The child pointed his finger up to the sky. Believing his son was mocking him, Shivapada raised his hand to discipline him. To his surprise, the toddler, who had, until recently been babbling, started singing in chaste Tamil.

thOdudaiya cheviyan vidaiyERi yOr thUveN madhichUdi
kAdudaiya chudalaip podipUchi yen uLLam kavarkaLvan
Edudaiya malarAn munain^At paNin^dhEththa aruLcheydha
pIdudaiya piramA pura mEviya pemmAn ivananRE

Wearing a ring in his ear, sitting on a bull, wearing a moon,
Covered with ash from the cremation ground, wearing flowers.
The Lord of Brahma came and stole my heart. That is who gave me milk.
(Thevaram, 1st Tirumurai, Tirugnanasambandar)

That child, who received divine milk, which assuaged his hunger and granted him the greatest knowledge, came to be known as Jnana Sambandar. He went on to become a revered saint, spreading Shiva bhakti across the people of Tamil Nadu.

Shiva and Parvati's compassion extends to all. They are the divine parents for all of humanity. This is revealed through other stories as well.

It was a stormy night at Tiruchirappalli, Tamil Nadu. Rain had been pounding the area for several days. People were huddled in their homes, and businesses were closed. The river Kaveri was close to flooding. The boats that plied people and their goods across the river were all tied up on the banks.

In a house by the foot of the Malaikkottai or Rockfort temple, pregnant Ratnavati was in the throes of labour. Her woodseller husband, Sudhakaran, was distraught. He tried in vain to ease Ratnavati's pain. But every few minutes he would rush to the door and peek into the stormy darkness.

Ratnavati's mother lived on the other side of the river Kaveri. Word had been sent requesting her to come and help with the childbirth. However, the boats had stopped crossing due to the weather and her mother was stranded with no other way to attend the delivery.

Sudhakaran decided to seek help with some friends nearby. Informing his labouring wife, he ran out into the night. Alone and in acute agony, Ratnavati was losing all hope.

In desperation, she turned her eyes in the direction of the temple that she had diligently visited every day of her life and cried, "How can you abandon me?" Immediately, the door flew open, and her mother ran in.

"Amma, you came!" Ratnavati cried as relief flooded her. Her mother helped her deliver a healthy baby. As her mother cleaned up, Ratnavati nursed her child and sank into an exhausted sleep. After a few moments, she heard her husband's footsteps.

Sudhakaran glanced at the baby and exclaimed, "O Ratnavati, you gave birth by yourself. Such extraordinary bravery!" Her mother, who had arrived with him cried, "Oh, my dear, I was so worried I wouldn't make it on time. I am so relieved that you delivered without me."

Ratnavati was perplexed. Was she hallucinating in her post-delivery fatigue? She looked at the baby happily sleeping in her arms, and surveyed the room, now clean and organized. She whispered, "What are you blabbering about, Amma? You came right before I delivered. How could I have delivered the baby by myself and cleaned up everything?"

Her mother emphatically denied it. "There were no boats. I had to walk all the way to the village and cajole a boatman with extra money to bring me once the rains slowed. How could I have come earlier?"

They stared at each other, baffled. The answer came to Ratnavati in a flash. "I know who came to my aid, disguised as you. Who else has the compassion and the power to do it?" Tears streamed down their faces as they turned their eyes in the direction of the temple atop that one billion years old rock.

Muthuswami Dikshitar, one of the Carnatic music trinity composers, extols the wonder of the Lord coming as a Vaishya-jati mother.

vaiśya jāti stri vesha dharaṇaṃ

One who assumed the role of a woman of the Vaishya jati.
(*Sri Matrbhutam*, Muthuswami Dikshitar)

Matrubhuteshwara, the Lord who is also Mother, is worshipped in the beautiful cave on Rockfort hill.

Sources: *Sirkazhi* (Brahmapuram, Tamil Nadu) *Sthala Puranam* and *Matrubhuteshwarar* (Tiruchirappalli, Tamil Nadu) *Sthala Puranam*

Fig. 14.1 Jnana Sambandar with his father at the Sirkazhi temple, Tamil Nadu
Source: https://cultureandheritage.org/

15

Mahabaleshwara

Ravana's mother, Kaikasi, was an ardent Shiva bhakta and can be credited with passing Shiva bhakti on to her infamous son. She ritualistically made a Parthiva Linga, out of sand, on the seashore and offered puja to it every day. Often, the waves would wash it away before her puja ended.

Ravana, despite his faults, was a dutiful son. Aware of her plight, he decided to get the Atma Linga for his mother. He had heard that this linga contained the prana, the life force, of Mahadeva.

Within minutes, his Pushpaka vimana, his flying chariot, took him to Kailasha, where he commenced his tapas to receive the Atma Linga from Sadashiva. Ravana possessed the rare ability to perform harsh penance, putting his body through immense hardships to attain his goal. Mahadeva had to appear and accede to his request.

Shiva blessed Ravana. "I will bestow the Atma Linga upon you. Wherever it is installed will become unconquerable. Those who worship it will become invincible." Ravana was thrilled. Not only would his mother gain this special linga, but Lanka would become indomitable by its presence.

Shiva was not done, though. He laid out a condition. The Atma Linga had to be carried in person and transported by foot. Once put down on the ground, it could not be lifted again. For the mighty Ravana, this was not an arduous task.

Ravana prostrated to Shiva, accepted the Atma Linga in his arms, and started walking south. He was filled with possibilities and plans for its installation in Lanka.

Indra could not accept such power being given so freely to Ravana. Fearing Lanka's invincibility, he sought Mahavishnu's help. The latter provided him with a novel solution. He invoked Ganesha and asked for his help in tricking Ravana.

"Much as we all dislike Ravana, to his credit, he never misses his Nithya karmas. Near sunset, he is bound to stop to perform his Sandhyaradhana. Ganesha, that is when you must grab the linga from him," Vishnu explained his strategy.

As Ravana was walking past the western seashore in today's Karnataka, Mahavishnu caused a fake sunset. Ravana was taken aback. He had not expected the sun to set so soon. He wondered how he was going to perform his Sandhyaradhana while holding the Atma Linga.

Ravana was alone on the seashore. He desperately looked around for someone to help him. He chanced upon a young Brahmana boy at some distance. Ravana ran to him.

"I need to do my Sandhya worship. Can you please hold this linga while I perform it?" Ravana pleaded with the reluctant boy.

"Ok, I will hold it, but don't take too long," the boy said as he received the linga.

Ravana rushed into the water and started offering *arghyam* to the sun. It was not many minutes before the boy cried out. "Sir, your linga is quite heavy. I cannot carry it for long. Please finish your worship."

Ravana was engrossed in his worship and did not hear the boy's calls. In a few minutes, Ravana finished his Sandhya Vandanam and turned. He was aghast to find the Atma Linga on the seashore, with the boy casually standing by it.

Ravana's disappointment at losing the Atma Linga turned into fury at the young boy. He caught hold of the boy to punish him. As he hit hard on the boy's forehead, Ganesha revealed his true form. And the sky became bright again.

Ravana realized he had been tricked by the devas. Running to the Atma Linga, he tried to pull it out. As Ravana tugged at it, the linga sunk further into the ground, shattering the casket, sending its pieces flying. The casket fell at Sajjeshwara, the cloth covering it flew to Murudeshwara, the string tying the cloth dropped at Dhareshwara, and the lid of the casket fell at Gunavanteshwara.

The place where Ganesha set down the Atma Linga came to be called Go-karna (cow's ear). The linga is buried in the ground and only its top, resembling a cow's ear, is visible. This unmovable linga came to be called the Mahabaleshwara—the Most Powerful Lord.

The five places are collectively known as the "Pancha Linga kshetras". The Ganesha in Gokarna still has a dent where Ravana struck him.

The Atma Linga that would have made Ravana more of a menace to the world now blesses countless devotees. This story reveals how Shiva can be bound by love, humility, and good intentions, not selfish and egoistic goals.

Ravana recognized his weaknesses and prayed for single-minded Shiva bhakti in his popular *Shiva Tandava Stotram.*

kadā nilimpanirjharīnikuñjakōṭarē vasan
vimuktadurmatiḥ sadā śiraḥsthamañjaliṃ vahan |
vimuktalōlalōchanō lalāṭaphālalagnakaḥ
śivēti mantramuchcharan sadā sukhī bhavāmyaham

When will I live a life of pleasure, meditating on Shiva,
Sitting near a hollow place near the celestial river Ganga,
Releasing all my ill thoughts with hands clasped above my head,
After releasing all passion for pretty women with shifting eyes?
(*Shiva Tandava Stotram*, verse 13, Ravana)

Source: *Gokarna Mahabaleshwara Sthala Puranam*

The Kotirudra Samhita in *Shiva Purana* makes a brief mention of Gokarna Mahabaleshwara:

ghoreṇa tapasā labdhaṃ rāvaṇākhyena rakṣasā |
talliṃgaṃ sthāpayāmāsa gokarṇa gaṇanāyakaḥ ||

The linga secured by the rakshasa Ravana as a result of severe penance was installed by Gaṇanayaka at Gokarṇa.

16

Jambukeshwara

A noisy squabble between two Gandharvas, Pushpadanta and Malyavan, was disrupting the serenity of Kailasha. The Shiva ganas engaged in puja, and the rishis in deep meditation sighed in frustration. This annoyance was not unprecedented. The two Shiva bhaktas were constantly bickering.

It is surprising when we face the stories of devas, rishis, and great bhaktas fighting like immature humans. Such is the hold of our vasanas—our innate tendencies—on our minds.

On that fateful day, the fight took a vicious turn. In blind rage, Malyavan cursed Pushpadanta. "You do not deserve to be a Gandharva. You will be born as an elephant!"

Pushpadanta now had to surpass this curse. He retorted, "Is that so? Then, you will be born as a spider, that I will trample on!"

They both were born in a great Shiva kshetram called Jambukeshwaram, in today's Tiruchirappalli in Tamil Nadu.

Legend goes, eons ago, momentarily bored by Shiva's constant meditation, Devi Parvati taunted him like a complaining wife. To remind her of the value of meditation, he sent her to do penance on earth.

Devi assumed the form of Akhilandeshwari, the goddess cradling the entire universe in her womb. She installed a linga on the banks of Kaveri, using water from the temple pond, the Brahma pushkarini, under the shade of a Jambu (rose apple) tree, and devotedly performed penance there. That linga came to be known as Jambukeshwaram.

The cursed Gandharvas, Pushpadanta and Malyavan, were born as an elephant and a spider, respectively, at this sacred place. Their intense Shiva bhakti continued in these new bodies, just as Adi Shankaracharya requests for all devotees.

naratvaṃ dēvatvaṃ naga-vana-mṛgatvaṃ maśakatā
paśutvaṃ kīṭatvaṃ bhavatu vihagatvādi-jananam
sadā tvat-pādābja-smaraṇa-paramānanda-laharī
vihārāsaktaṃ chēd-hṛdayaṃ-iha kiṃ tēna vapuśā

Be it as a human, a deva, a forest creature, a mountain animal, or even a mosquito,
Be it a cow or a worm, a bird, or whichever body we take,
What does it matter as long as the mind is always engaged.
In the meditation of your lotus feet, which are the waves of supreme bliss,
(*Shivananda Lahari*, verse 10, Adi Shankaracharya)

Regrettably, along with their Shiva bhakti, their enmity also persisted in their new forms. This illustrates how our innate tendencies, or vasanas, can transcend lifetimes.

Every day, the elephant would fetch water from the river Kaveri and perform *abhishekam* to Shiva Linga under the Jambu tree. Simultaneously, the spider would construct an intricate web above the linga to shield it from debris. However, every morning, the elephant, oblivious to the spider's devotion, would wash away the web, deeming it dirt. The spider would reweave the web again.

This futile cycle repeated until, one day, the enraged spider crawled into the trunk of the elephant and bit its insides. In throbbing pain, the elephant thrashed around, smashing his trunk against a rock in an attempt to rid himself of the spider. However, in the process, he ended up hurting himself fatally and both eventually died. Pashupati, torn between appreciation for their devotion and annoyance at their discord, mercifully released them from the curse.

Jambukeshwara, known in Tamil as Thiru-Aanai-Kaa, earned its name the "holy forest of the elephant" as an elephant worshipped Shiva here. Residing on the waters of Kaveri, the linga is recognized as the Water Linga or Apu Linga, one of the five elements or *pancha bhuta* lingas. Today, the sanctum perpetually receives water from the Kaveri.

Yugas later, during the reign of an early Chola king, Kochengannan, in the 1st century BCE, Subadevan and his wife Kamalavati prayed to Lord Nataraja for a son. Blessed by the Lord, Malyavan, his spider devotee, was born to them. The child was born with red eyes. Hence, he was called Kochengannan, the red-eyed king.

Continuing his Shiva bhakti, Kochengannan built nearly 70 temples, the magnificent Jambukeshwaram temple being one of them. Later, Vijayanagara rulers expanded the temple to its sprawling grandeur today.

Parashara Rishi has composed *Jambukeshwara Stotram*, narrating the birth of this miraculous kshetram, with mentions of the elephant and spider. It is believed that Parashara Rishi visited this kshetram to perform a yagna for the auspicious journey, sadgati, of his departed father. However, considering the mention of the 1st century BCE Chola king, it may have been composed by another bhakta who attributed it to Parashara Rishi.

sonākśa chola kṛta gopura sauḍaśāla
sanmaṇtapojjwalaradhanaa vana sthitāya
ūrnāya tantumaya mandira vāsine prāk
śri jambu mūla nilayāya namaśivāya ||

I salute Lord Shiva, who sits below a jambu (rose apple) tree,
who lives in the forest of elephants,
In a temple built by the Chola king Sonaksha
(Kochengannan),
which has a huge gopura, corridors, and bright mantapas
who stays under a net woven by spiders.
(*Jambukeshwara Ashtakam*, verse 4, Parashara Rishi)

As the compassionate Pashupati, Lord Jambukeshwara, and his consort Akhilandeshwari, will bless all with Shiva bhakti.

Source: *Gajaranya Mahatmyam*

Fig. 16. 1 Shiva Linga under a Jambu tree worshipped by Parvati as Akhilandeshwari. The elephant does abhishekam while the spider weaves a web above. Carving on a pillar in Tiruvanaikkaval, Trichy, Tamil Nadu

Source: https://ancientterminus.com/

Arunachala

During Maha Pralaya, the great deluge, creation dissolved into nothingness, and the five elements, the sun or moon did not yet exist. There was no day, night, or time. There were no universes or creatures. It was before the devas, the saptarishis, or the prajapatis had been created. The formless and changeless Parabrahman, the eternal consciousness prevailed.

Parabrahman transformed into Sadashiva. From his Shakti emerged the mahat tattva. They were further divided into twenty-four tattvas, the building blocks of creation. The sattva guna of Sadashiva manifested as Mahavishnu. Mahavishnu rested on an endless snake, Adi Shesha, on the milky ocean, the Ksheera Sagara. Through his yoga maya, Mahavishnu performed unseen miracles.

A lotus stemmed from Mahavishnu's navel, extending for countless yojanas, and ending in a mammoth lotus bud. As the pralaya waters calmed, it bloomed into a magnificent giant lotus, with thousands of radiant petals, hundreds of yojanas wide. On the huge golden carpel at its centre, a new radiant being emerged, shining with five heads.

Thus emerged Brahma, endowed with knowledge of the Vedas and a sankalpa—an inborn desire—to create. He manifested the Prajapatis and imbued them with his creative impulse. They propagated thousands of species.

Unique creatures started appearing in the universe. They continued to multiply, rapidly populating the worlds.

Brahma watched the progress, proud of his creations. "Such a dazzling range of devas, asuras, gandharvas, naras, birds, and beasts. I have created them all."

Brahma decided to take a stroll out of his lotus. Standing atop the highest petal, he saw the milky ocean stretching below. As he followed the lotus stem, he chanced upon the hood of a humongous snake, curled around itself, floating on the ocean. He descended further and, on the coiled snake, saw a beautiful blue presence stretched out in blissful slumber.

Brahma approached him to strike up a conversation, but the blue entity did not stir. Brahma clapped his hands to awaken him. Mahavishnu opened his eyes languidly, like the gentle bloom of a wet lotus.

"When an honourable person visits, one must welcome them with arghyam, not sleep carelessly. I am Brahma, the creator of this magnificent universe. How dare you do not heed my presence?" Brahma said, waving his hand to display his creation.

Vishnu sat up, beaming. "Oh, Brahma, my child, you are the universe's creator. And I am Mahavishnu, your creator."

His burgeoning pride was wounded by this declaration. Brahma cried, "How can you be my creator? Nonsense. I am the only creator. Let me show you who is greater!" He launched himself into a duel with Vishnu.

A battle for supremacy ensued. Furious, Brahma launched the terrible Pashupata astra on Vishnu, who responded with the scorching Maheshwara astra. The intensity of this warfare caused tremendous quakes across the planets.

The devas recognized the futility of this war. They knew that the supreme Parabrahman was the only cause of creation. The devas ran to Sadashiva to stop this childish war between the two devatas. Sadashiva smiled and vanished.

The two devatas Vishnu and Brahma, engrossed in battle, found their eyes blinded by an effulgence. They turned their gaze at the huge, dazzling column of fire, radiant like a thousand suns that had suddenly appeared. This shocking sight moved them to pause their battle.

Brahma had hitherto thought himself to be all knowing. This new phenomenon shook his self-esteem. "What is this fire? Where did it come from? How far does it go?" he asked in a shaken voice.

"I don't know, but I will find out." He turned to Brahma and continued, "This may be a way to end our duel. Whoever finds the source or end of this column of fire first will be declared supreme. Do you agree?" Brahma nodded.

Vishnu took the form of Varaha, the boar, and dived down to find the bottom end of the fire, while Brahma transformed into a majestic swan and flew up to find the upper end. Eons passed, but the search proved to be futile. Mahavishnu decided to give up and return to his abode. Brahma, tired yet prideful, refused to concede to Vishnu.

As he was pondering his next steps, he was hit by a strong fragrance. Looking up, he saw a flower floating down adjacent to the column. As it drifted nearer, he recognized it as a ketaki flower (crepe ginger). An idea struck him. He sought and gained the support of the flower to bear false witness to his victory. They flew back to their starting point, where he found Vishnu lounging on his Adi Shesha.

With a smirk, Brahma clapped his hands and woke him up again. "Vishnu, you are such a quitter. I persisted and found the top of the column of fire. See, I brought back this ketaki as proof."

Vishnu, humbled, admitted defeat. He said, "You are indeed superior, Brahma. I gave up a while back. In any case, I was wrong to be proud. After all, you and I but manifest the powers of Parabrahman." Brahma secretly gloated at successfully tricking Vishnu.

A thunderous sound erupted from that light column and resounded across the universe. The brightness in the middle of the column revealed an angry white face with three eyes, framed by a huge mass of dark, matted hair.

"Brahma, I, Sadashiva, endowed you with the Vedas, the greatest knowledge. I empowered you to create this brilliant world. Yet you not only take credit for it but also lie to Mahavishnu to claim victory over him. Shame on you!" Mahadeva thundered.

While Brahma cowered in shame, Mahavishnu spoke up with courage and honesty. "Lord, I had momentarily forgotten that it is your power that makes us create and protect the universe. Forgive us."

Shiva smiled at him. "It was my lila, my divine sport, to remind you and the world not to claim doership and pride for accomplishing any task. Vishnu, you recalled this and returned to the truth." His gaze turned to Brahma. "Brahma, you will never be worshipped, nor have temples or festivals devoted to you. And I shun the Ketaki flower from my worship forever."

Brahma lamented, "Lord, I was a fool. I cannot even create a blade of grass without your grace, but I flaunted what I thought was my creation. This pride also provoked me to lie. I will forever be ashamed, but please forgive me, so I may continue my creation task with confidence."

Shiva was willing to forgive the truly repentant. "Brahma, you will not have a temple. But you will be the presiding devata for all yagnas. O Ketaki, while I will not wear you, you will continue to be used for other devatas and bring fragrance to their worship."

The devas joined Mahavishnu and Brahma to glorify this Parabrahma swarupa, who is the light of consciousness that enlivens every part of creation.

This day was called Maha Shivaratri and Mahadeva imparted the secret of his worship to the world. "I, who am Nirakara, the formless, manifested as the column of fire. Henceforth this form will be worshipped in the form of a linga. Let all fast on this day and night and meditate upon me to understand my truth and reach me."

"My column of fire will also manifest as an incarnadine mountain—Arunachala. It will forever be sacred. For many yugas, it will attract devout seekers and bestow knowledge upon them," he blessed.

Since Bhagavan manifested as the column of light and fire, this kshetra in Tamil Nadu is a Pancha Bhuta sthala, and the linga is called the Agni Linga. Just as it taught Mahavishnu and Brahma the Parabrahma *tattvam*, Arunachala is an ever-present guru, guiding seekers to self-realization.

This hill was believed to be Sadashiva himself. Over eons, great yogis and siddhas arrived to live on its slopes, attracted by its divinity. Under the guidance of Gautama Rishi, Devi Gauri performed tapas here and merged into Shiva at this kshetra.

While many saints have wondered at the mystery of Arunachala, adored him from far, circumambulated him with veneration, and prayed to him for boons, none have singularly connected to him quite like Bhagavan Ramana Maharishi.

Venkataraman was a playful, ordinary boy growing up in Madurai. When he was sixteen, he had a near death experience. Instead of fearing it, he analysed what happens after death, inquired what would remain, and, through that self-enquiry, realized himself as the eternal Atman. Soon after that remarkable experience, a visitor to his house mentioned that he had been to Arunachala. The mention of that divine name led him to the kshetra.

He left home, boarded the train to Tiruvannamalai, went directly to the temple, surrendered to Arunachaleshwara, and never left the hill. He lived there to finally settle in the ashram, at the foothills of Arunachala. He has maintained that the hill is Shiva.

aRivaRu giriyena amartarum ammA
adisayam idanseyal aRivaridArkkum
aRivaru siruvayad adumudal aruNA
chalamigap peridena aRivin ilanga
aRigilan adanporuL adu tiruvaNNA
malaiyena oruvarAl aRivuRap peTRum
aRivinai maruLuRut aruginil eerkka
aruguRumamayamid achalamA kaNDEn

Look! There Arunachala stands
As if an insentient Mountain.
Yet, mysterious is the way it works,
beyond all human understanding.
From my unthinking childhood,
Arunachala had shone in my awareness.
When I heard its name, I did not realise its real meaning.
When it drew me to itself,
I saw that it was stillness absolute!
(*Arunachala Ashtakam*, verse 1, Bhagavan Ramana Maharishi)

In direct contrast to the vibrant, energetic Nataraja is the still, unchanging Arunachala—both manifestations of the same tattvam. One represents the ever-changing universe, while the other embodies the changeless foundation, the Atman itself.

That eternal and still Arunachaleshwara leads all to the realization of our eternal and still Shiva-self.

Source: Maheshwara Khanda and Arunachala Khanda, *Skanda Purana*

Fig. 17.1 Lingodbhava Murti at Airavateshwara Temple, Darasuram, 10th century CE. Column of fire, with Vishnu as Varaha, the boar, and Brahma, as a swan, flying up to find its ends. Shiva is manifesting in it

18

Somanatha

Imagine a kshetra—a sacred town—so ancient that Sri Krishna and the Pandavas worshipped there. This was the Prabhasa kshetra, referred to as Prabhasa Pattana in ancient texts and travelogues. Shiva claimed it as his favourite teertha sthala. For thousands of years, it has bustled with pilgrims from across Bharat and beyond. They came to worship at the Somnath Jyotirlinga and the eponymous Surya temple (Prabhasa meaning brilliance of the sun). Veraval port, nearby, attracted immense fame and wealth through travellers and traders. The city was associated with both Surya and Chandra, the sun, and the moon.

Eons ago, Chandra, or Soma, married the twenty-seven daughters of Daksha Prajapati (they are revered as the twenty-seven prime stars in ancient Hindu astronomy). Daksha, who had played favourites and disrespected his son-in-law Mahadeva, rather hypocritically demanded that Chandra treat all his wives equally. However, Soma was most attached to Rohini. Miffed, his other wives complained to their father. Daksha's repeated warnings could not decrease Soma's preference for Rohini.

Enraged, Daksha thundered, "Soma, it is a husband's duty to keep his wives happy. Despite my repeated warnings you have not rectified your behaviour. Your effulgence has made you arrogant. I curse that you will lose your light!" Before Chandra could defend himself, his light dimmed.

This punishment for Chandra was a catastrophe for the world. Humans could not travel at night, lovers could not nurture their romance, and medicinal herbs ceased to grow without the nourishing light of the moon.

Chandra, thus rendered helpless, turned to the compassionate Mahadeva. He worshipped the Shiva Linga at Prabhasa kshetra, performing penance by meditating on the Mrtyunjaya mantra for six months.

Pleased with his worship, Shiva appeared before him. "Soma, I am touched by your devotion. Henceforth, I shall be referred to as Somanath in this temple to honour your devotion. I cannot completely reverse Daksha's curse and restore your old brightness," he said to Chandra's dismay. "However, I can bless you to wane for a fortnight and grow again for a fortnight. This cycle will alternate between your complete brightness and your complete darkness (Purnima to Amavasya)."

With this blessing, the cycle of the moon was established, leading to variety in the night sky as well as tides in the ocean. Lord Shiva gained the name of Somanatha. Further still, Somavara (Monday), the day of the week dedicated to the moon, is considered the best day for Shiva puja across Bharat.

saurāṣṭradēśē viśadē'tiramyē jyōtirmayaṃ chandrakaḻāvataṃsam I
bhaktapradānāya kṛpāvatīrṇaṃ taṃ sōmanāthaṃ śaraṇaṃ prapadyē II

I seek refuge in the Somanatha, who is in the
holy and pretty Sourashtra,
who is dazzling with light, who wears the crescent of the moon,
and who has come there to give the gift of devotion and mercy.
(*Dwadasha Jyotirlinga Stotram*, Adi Shankaracharya)

There is a sad similarity between the moon and the Somnath temple itself. The Somnath temple endured seventeen known cycles of destruction by Islamic invaders. Yet it was rebuilt each time by devotees.

The first destruction was by Mahmud of Ghazni, who established the tradition of desecration and plunder of Hindu temples in 1026 CE. Fifty thousand devotees lost their lives trying to protect the temple but could not prevail against the frenzied iconoclasm of the invaders. Though they failed to defend the temple, they rebuilt it again.

Destruction of the restored Somnath temple became a tradition for Islamic invaders in every century with Ulugh Khan, Zafar Khan, and Mahmud Begada following in Mahmud of Ghazni's footsteps. Hindus, undeterred by destruction, restored it to its ancient glory every time.

The latest reconstruction led by Sardar Vallabhbhai Patel and K.M. Munshi symbolizes that while temples can be broken and murtis defaced, Shiva bhakti endures in India.

Source: Prabhasa Khanda, *Skanda Purana*

Fig. 18. 1 The earliest photo of Somnath taken by Sykes and Nelson, 1895

Fig. 18.2 The current Somnath temple reconstructed by Sardar Vallabhbhai Patel and K.M. Munshi. The architect is Prabhashankarbhai Oghadbhai Sompura of the Sompura Salat clan. The temple used a few of the sculptures recovered from the ruins of the old temple

19

Mallikarjuna

Life at Kailasha was idyllic. The father and mother of the universe, Jaganmata and Jagatpita, watched their brilliant sons, Ganesha and Kartikeya, learn, grow, play, and help protect the world. All rejoiced at the sight of this divine family.

Yet, the lila of Mahadeva is inexplicable and unpredictable, though wise people know that it always results in good for creation. Sibling rivalry raised its ugly head at Kailasha, much like in common households.

Like all parents in the world, Uma and Maheshwara started discussing their sons' marriages. Each brother clamoured to be married immediately. But how could they pick the first to be married? Mahadeva had an idea.

"Sons, we love you both equally. We cannot pick one of you over the other. I propose we have a race. Whoever goes around the earth seven times and returns first will be the first to be married. Do you agree?" he asked with a mischievous smile. Kartikeya enthusiastically nodded his head, and Ganapati followed suit, albeit more thoughtfully.

To the great warrior, Kartikeya, who had destroyed the savage hordes of Surapadma, Simhamukha, and Taraka, this contest was trivial. In addition, he had a powerful peacock vahana to cover long distances. With a smirk at his brother, he straddled his peacock and flew off.

On the other hand, Ganapati was cerebral. He always avoided intense activity if he could manage it. Further, his vahana was the mushika, the mouse, with no gift of speed. Ganesha paced around his parents, pondering. That's it. His large eyes glinted, and he waved his trunk in joy. He approached his parents, bowed before them, and then walked around them (in pradakshina) seven times. Shiva and Parvati were bemused.

Parvati spoke, concerned, "Dear child, why have you not left to circumambulate the earth? I realize you are at a disadvantage, but will you not even try?"

The clever Ganesha explained, "Mother, why do you ask this question when I have already circumambulated you, not once, but seven times? Don't the shastras say that one's parents are equal to the world? If that is the case for all parents, then it must be unquestionably true for you both, the mother and father of the universe. By circling you both, I have won the race. If you don't accept this logic, the Vedas will be proven wrong!"

His stunned parents could not deny his logic and beamed at his intelligence.

Immediately, wedding preparations were underway. Prajapati Vishwarupa offered Siddhi and Buddhi, his two lovely daughters, as brides. Without much delay, the wedding was organized. In quick succession, two sons named Kshema and Laabha were born to Siddhi and Buddhi, respectively. So much happened in the faster divine calendar while Kartikeya was intently circling the earth.

Finally, Kartikeya returned to Kailasha, confident that he had won the race. To his shock, he found that his brother had married and even had children. while he was still racing. In what way was this fair? His young face reddened with rage and humiliation.

Narada added fuel to his anger. "How can you live with parents who deliberately tricked you?" He provoked the young Kumara. Narada's plans, however diabolical they sounded, were always for the welfare of the world.

Disappointed with his parents, Kartikeya renounced Kailasha and retreated to Krauncha Hill. There was a deeply sacred vibe on this sacred hill which has been equated with Kashi and Arunachala in the Puranas.

Parvati could not bear his angry departure. She cajoled Maheshwara to accompany her to Krauncha and convince Kartikeya to return.

They tried to assuage his anger. "This is childish, my son. This race was simply Ishwara lila. Can we, as parents, play favourites among both of you? Come back to Kailasha with us. We will get you married." But Kartikeya remained firm in his denial. "I will not return. If you miss me, you can visit me here," he categorically said, seated on the branch of an Arjuna tree.

The concerned parents themselves decided to visit and check on Kartikeya regularly. Mahadeva visited every Amavasya (new moon day), and Parvati visited every Purnima (full moon day). They both liked the picturesque place nestled in the Nallamalai Hills of contemporary Andhra

Pradesh. Here, the river Krishna descended into a deep valley called the Patala Ganga.

A sliver of the jyotirlinga had manifested as a Swayambhu (self-manifest) Linga under an Arjuna tree (Terminalia Arjuna) on this hill. A lovely jasmine creeper wound itself around the tree and showered its fragrant blossoms on the linga. Hence, the linga was called Mallikarjuna Mahalingam.

This is a Shakti peetha as well since Dakshayini's neck fell here after the destruction of the Daksha yagam. In another legend here, she took the form of Bhramarambika (a bee) to kill the demon Arunasura. Great rishis and kings have been drawn to this kshetra for eons.

The historical epigraphy in this temple dates to the 2nd century CE. The Satavahanas, Vishnukundis, Chalukyas, and Kakatiyas built and expanded the temple. Rani Ahilyabai Holkar, the notable temple patron of recent times, also renovated the temple further and built the ghat.

Bhagavan Adi Shankaracharya meditated by the twin falls near the temple and sang the intellectually brilliant and emotionally moving Shivanandalahari. His enriching presence there is immortalized by a small temple. In his poetry, he mentions the beautiful couple, who reside there, Bhramarambika and Mallikarjuna, who live atop the Sri Giri (a synonym for Sri Shailam, its present name).

sandhyārambha-vijṛmbhitaṃ śruti-śira-sthānāntar-ādhiśṭhitaṃ
sa-prēma bhramarābhirāmam-asakṛt sad-vāsanā-śōbhitam
bhōgīndrābharaṇaṃ samasta-sumanaḥ-pūjyaṃ guṇāviśkṛtaṃ
sēvē śrī-giri-mallikārjuna-mahā-lingaṃ śivālingitaṃ

He who enjoys dancing in the evening, He who lives in the Upanishads,
He who is deeply in love with Bhramarambika,
He who always has the scent of the devotion of the sages,
He who wears the king of snakes as an ornament,
He who is worshipped by all with a good mind,
He who is known for his good qualities,
I serve that Mallikarjuna who lives atop the Srigiri.
(*Shivanandalahari*, verse 50, Adi Shankaracharya)

Another fervent devotee, Akka Mahadevi, a prominent Veerashaiva saint, ardently yearned for union with Chenna Mallikarjuna. Forsaking possessions and relationships, she roamed naked and entered the Anubhava Mantapa of the Veerashaivas of Karnataka

The head of the anubhava mantapa, Allama Prabhu, assumed she was insane. He stopped her and queried, "Why have you come here, O young woman? Who is your husband?"

Without hesitation, she proclaimed her husband to be Lord Chenna Mallikarjuna, the lord of Sri Sailam. When Allama Prabhu asked about the identity of her earthly husband, she sang,

Ihakkobba gandane parakkobba gandane?
Laukikakkobba gandane pAramArthakkobba gandane?
yenna ganda chennamallikArjuna devaralladhe
mikkina gandarella mugila mareya bombeyanthe

Should there be one husband in this
world and another in heaven?
Should there be one husband for worldly purposes and
another for spiritual purposes?
My husband is none other than Lord Chenna Mallikarjuna.
All other husbands are like puppets hidden in the sky.
(Akka Mahadevi's vachanas)

The fragrant grace of Mallikarjuna will lead us into Shiva-ananda-lahari—the waves of bliss of Shiva.

Sources: Kotirudra Samhita (*Shiva Purana*) and *Srisailam Sthala Purana*

There is a variation to this legend of competition between Ganesha and Kartikeya in the Sthala Purana of Palani in Tamil Nadu. In this instance, the competition was for a divine mango. Ganesha employed the same cunning short cut of circumambulating Shiva-Parvati, thereby winning the mango. Kartikeya left, enraged, and settles in present day Palani hill in Tamil Nadu.

Source: *Palani Sthala Puranam*

20

Bhimashankara

On the slopes of the Sahyadri hills, a young rakshasa called Bhima grew up with his mother, Karkati. As he entered his youth, curiosity about his father, typical of any fatherless child, consumed him.

One day, Bhima, eager for answers, prompted Karkati to share the story of her past. "I was born to rakshasa parents. and married to Viradha, a rakshasa who roamed the Dandaka Forest, causing havoc. One day, he made the fatal mistake of snatching Sita, the wife of Rama, the prince of Ayodhya. Consequently, Viradha paid with his life." Her voice cracked with sorrow.

Bhima nudged her to continue. She resumed, "Thus widowed, I returned home to live with my parents. However, they too were killed by Rishi Sutikshna for their transgressions. Utterly alone, I tried to survive in these hills. One day, Kumbhakarna, the brother of Ravana, the King of Lanka, saw me bathing in a pond. He forced himself upon me. You were born soon after."

Bhima was saddened by his mother's tribulations. Yet intrigued by the greatness of his father, Kumbhakarna, he asked her, "Where is my father? Can I see him?"

Karkati, aware of Kumbhakarna's fate in the Rama–Ravana war informed him that Rama had killed his father as well.

The revelation turned Bhima's hope to anguish, fuelling a fierce anger against the world, Vishnu, the devas, the rishis, and the kings for denying him his right to a father. With his mother's blessings, he undertook intense tapas for years, seeking invincibility. When Brahma appeared before him, he had to grant Bhima his desired boon, for even the creator was bound by the laws of karma.

Thus empowered, Bhima went on a violent spree, conquering Indraloka and imprisoning the devas. Then he wreaked havoc on earth. He pursued rishis and munis, forcing them to flee from Sahyadri to Kamarupa, the kingdom of King Sudakshina, an ardent Shiva bhakta.

However, Bhima followed them there and captured the king and his wife. The royal couple were thrown into an isolated cell. All the rishis and brahmanas were subjected to torture.

Despite their adversities, King Sudakshina and his wife Dakshina maintained their unwavering devotion to Mahadeva. Bhakti does not change according to situations. Sudakshina whispered to his wife, "Devi, everything that happens is our prarabhdha—our destiny due to past karmas. The only thing we have control over is our present actions. We must continue our worship of Mahadeva. Shivaradhana is our goal, our bliss, and our support." Dakshina was of the same mind.

They shaped the mud in their cell into a Parthiva Linga (a linga made of earth) and worshipped it with complete devotion. Though they lacked the material offerings for a proper puja, their thoughts were pure and focused on Shiva.

Meanwhile, Bhima continued to ravage the earth, stopping yagnas and defiling the Vedas. One day, one of his rakshasa guards alerted Bhima about King Sudakshina's supposed black magic intended to kill him.

Bhima immediately confronted the King. "What kind of black magic are you doing? What is this?" He roared, pointing at the Parthiva Linga.

The king answered, calmed by the strength of his bhakti. "This is Shiva Linga, the symbol of my Lord Mahadeva. He is Pashupati, the protector of all. I am simply seeking his protection for my people."

Bhima thundered in rage, "I have heard about Mahadeva. He is a naked yogi meditating all the time. What can your Lord do to me?" He thrust his sword at the linga trying to destroy it.

As the sword touched the linga, Rudra blazed forth from it, enraged by the abuse of his devotees. A fierce battle ensued between Rudra and Bhima. Rudra wielded his bow, the Pinaka, to shatter Bhima's weapons, one after another. Two Shiva ganas, Dakini and Sakini, joined the fray. The battle seemed unending.

Eventually, Rudra's sigh—*hum-kara*—burnt Bhima to ashes. As a result of the prolonged battle, Mahadeva had perspired profusely. His sweat became the river Bhima. The rishis beseeched Mahadeva to abide forever in that kshetra as Bhimashankara, for the benefit of humanity. The kshetra now stands in the verdant Sahyadri, with a new temple built by the Marathas.

yaṃ ḍākiniśākinikāsamājē niṣēvyamāṇaṃ piśitāśanaiścha ।
sadaiva bhīmādipadaprasiddhaṃ taṃ śaṅkaraṃ bhaktahitaṃ namāmi ॥

I salute that Lord Sankara Who is the darling of his devotees,
Who is being worshipped by rakshasas,
In the company of Ghosts called Dakini and Sakini,
And who is well known as "Bheema".
(*Dwadasha Jyotirlinga Stotram*, Adi Shankaracharya)

Our Manasa puja to Bhimashankara protects us from egoistic opponents, both within and outside ourselves.

Source: Kotirudra Samhita, chapter 20–21, *Shiva Purana*

21

Grishneshwara

In the hills of present-day Maharashtra, a devout brahmana called Sudharma lived a life steeped in rituals, dedicating himself to Shiva. He performed all the prescribed rituals, from the daily Sandhya Vandana to Shiva pujas, with complete surrender. With Sadashiva in his heart, he had attained complete detachment from worldly possessions.

His wife, Sudeha, hailed from a Shiva bhakta lineage. She was a pillar of support for her husband in his karmas. Yet, she harboured deep sorrow due to their childlessness. However, her husband did not share her sentiments. He tried to console her by saying, "My dear, let us accept Mahadeva's will and direct our lives to Shiva bhakti." But this did not comfort her. Instead, her desire to be a mother only grew stronger over time, fanned by neighbours who mocked her barrenness.

She beseeched her husband to seek Shiva's boon for a son. When initial prayers did not yield the desired result, Sudharma turned to his wife and said, "Our preordained destiny due to the karma from our past lives cannot be changed. Let us not pursue this any further and turn to serving Mahadeva instead."

When desire transforms into an unyielding craving, reason vanishes and knowledge dissipates, paving the path to imminent destruction. Sudeha had been struck by this affliction.

dhyāyato viṣhayān puṁsaḥ saṅgas teṣhūpajāyate
saṅgāt sañjāyate kāmaḥ kāmāt krodho 'bhijāyate
krodhād bhavati sammohaḥ sammohāt smṛiti-vibhramaḥ
smṛiti-bhranśhād buddhi-nāśho buddhi-nāśhāt praṇaśhyati

While contemplating on the objects of the senses, one develops attachment to them. Attachment leads to desire, and from desire arises anger. Anger leads to clouding of judgment, which results in bewilderment of memory. When memory is bewildered, the intellect gets destroyed; and when the intellect is destroyed, one is ruined (Bhagavad Gita 2.62–63).

She urged her husband. "Since I cannot have a child, I want you to take another wife." Sudharma vehemently refused, anticipating further complications in the future. "Wife, now you suffer from an unmet desire. If you bring another woman into our family and she succeeds to bear a child, you will suffer from jealousy as well."

Sudeha, in her stubbornness, brought home her younger sister, Ghushma. She argued, "I might come to envy other women, but not my own sister. Please marry her and fulfil my desire for a son for the family."

Tired of this marital discord, Sudharma acceded to his wife's request. However, he soon discovered that his new wife was a blessing to the family.

Sudeha's younger sister, Ghushma, was a devout Shiva bhakta. She was governed by the singular desire to worship Sadashiva. Every morning, she would gather mud from a nearby pond and craft one hundred and one Shiva Lingas.

She would worship them all with unwavering devotion, ending her day by immersing these lingas in the same pond. Over the years, she had worshipped over a hundred thousand Shiva Lingas.

Mahadeva, recognizing her sincere bhakti, bestowed upon her a handsome, intelligent, and noble son. This happy occasion birthed contrasting emotions in the family. Joy filled Sudharma, for despite his dispassion, the Lord had blessed him with a son. However, as predicted, Sudeha was infected with envy. When Ghushma placed the smiling baby on Sudeha's lap, her sister recoiled, averting her gaze.

Ghushma's tranquil countenance contrasted sharply with her sister's reaction. She believed her son belonged to Mahadeva, that her Lord had willed this radiant child into existence. There was nothing to celebrate when something was given and nothing to lament when it was taken away. Shiva bhakti had already moulded her into a Sthita-prajna, a person of steady self-knowledge.

This child grew up rapidly, earning resounding praises from friends and family alike. These compliments further festered the wound in Sudeha's heart. It filled her with hatred towards the world. She shunned the son that she had gone to such extreme lengths to bring into their lives. Ghushma often reminded Sudeha of their son's shared parentage, insisting that she was as much his mother as Ghushma was. The son, too, was loving and respectful towards Sudeha. Yet, none of it eased the torment of her heart.

Her spite turned into malevolence when the son married a rich, beautiful girl. The more adulation the couple received, the darker Sudeha's mind became. Thoughts of their ruin haunted her waking moments, robbing her of sleep or rest.

One night, in the thrall of this unrelenting darkness within her, she did something heinous. She quietly grabbed a curved axe and murdered the young man as he slept. Sudeha shoved the hacked body into a sack, dragged it outside, and threw it into the pond where his mother, Ghushma, had immersed the innumerable worshipped Shiva Lingas over the years.

At the next sunrise, while Sudharma and Ghusma were midway through their daily morning ablutions and Shiva puja, they heard the panic-stricken shriek of the young wife. She had discovered blood and fragments of her husband's body in his bed. Her wails shook the house. Sudeha joined in with the laments.

Despite the gruesome discovery, Sudharma and Ghushma continued their puja, unperturbed. Ghushma reached out to Shiva, "You created the boy, and you will protect him. You know how best to cultivate us jeevas in this garden you've planted. I embrace your will. I have nothing to worry about."

She finished her puja and calmly immersed her Shiva Lingas in the pond. When she looked up, she saw her son rising from the waters and walking towards her, unscathed. Ghushma embraced her son with her usual tranquil certainty, accepting this too as Mahadeva's will.

Shiva was overcome with the urge to bless these rare devotees. He manifested in that pond and said, "Ghushma, mahatmas of your ilk are extremely rare. I protect people like you. Those who seek to harm you need to be punished. I will punish Sudeha for her crime."

Ghushma fell to her knees at this resplendent vision and spoke, "Please let my sister live. Like many before her, she was ensnared by desire. The sight of your glorious form will purify her. Please purify this place with your presence and all devotees who seek you."

Mahadeva said with a smile, "Here, I shall manifest as a jyotirlinga and be known by your name, as Ghushmeshwara. This pond filled with lingas will be called Shivalaya. Those who worship here will be blessed with purity and happiness." A dazzling jyotirlinga appeared near the pond.

Sudeha, redeemed by Shiva darshana, and Sudharma, moved by Ghushma's devotion, circumambulated the linga. The transformative power of Shiva bhakti guided Sudeha towards atonement, freeing her from the depths of evil.

ilāpurē ramyaviśālakēsmin samullasantaṃ cha jagadvarēṇyam
vandē mahōdāratarasvabhāvaṃ ghṛṣṇēśvarākhyaṃ śaraṇaṃ prapadyē

I seek the refuge of Ghrshneshwara,
who lives and plays in the pretty city of Ilapura,
who is the greatest in the universe, and who is by nature extremely kind.
(*Dwadasha Jyotirlinga Stotram,* Adi Shankaracharya)

Unwavering meditation on Ghushmeshwara invokes self-awareness akin to Ghushma.

Source: Kotirudra Samhita, *Shiva Purana*

22

Rameshwara

Rama's war with Ravana, a saga of some length and much gore, culminated in an auspicious end. Ravana was vanquished. Sita was rescued. Lanka's throne was passed on to Vibheeshana. It was time for Rama, the prince of Ayodhya, to return home. They boarded the Pushpaka Vimana and crossed the ocean. As they flew over the Gandhamadana hill, Rama decided to stop. On this hill, Rama had prayed to Mahadeva prior to the war. He explained the significance of the place to Sita.

atra pūrve mahādevah
prasādam ākarot prabhuh

At this place, Lord Shiva formerly bestowed his grace on me.
(Yuddha Kanda, book vi, chapter 123, verse 19, Valmiki Ramayana)

Rishis arrived there to pay homage to Rama. They lauded him for ridding the world of demons. Yet Rama, a staunch follower of Dharma, seemed troubled.

He bowed down to the rishis. "O Sages, though my cause was just, the slaying of Ravana, Rishi Pulastya's grandson, imposes the burden of brahma hatya upon me," he said.

His entourage met this revelation with surprised gazes. They turned to Sita, expecting her to challenge this. But her serene countenance affirmed alignment with Rama on views of Dharma.

Ravana bore brahmana lineage. He was the son of Rishi Vishravas and Kaikasi. Ravana became a Vedic scholar, immersed in Shiva bhakti. Sadly, these qualities could not sublimate his ego, lust, and thirst for power. It seemed counterintuitive to repent ending the menace that dared to abduct Rama's wife.

Undeterred by their reaction, Rama declared, "Worship of Mahadeva purifies all paapa, even brahma hatya. Tell me, revered sages, how do I purge my sin?"

Their counsel was simple yet profound. "Install a Shiva Linga and worship the Lord at this sacred kshetra. Eons ago, when Shiva appeared as an endless pillar of light, this place became a jyotirlinga kshetra. Worship here and the linga shall match the sanctity of Vishwanatha in Kashi."

Rama's eyes lit up. He sought out Hanuman, who was ever eager to do Rama-kaaj—the work of Rama.

"Hanuman, please secure a Swayambhu Linga from Kailasha. Two auspicious muhurtas remain today. Nobody but you can accomplish this task within this time frame," he requested.

Enthused by the honour of such a task, Hanuman flexed his legs and soared to Kailasha. But the hill, usually teeming with lingas, seemed baren that day. Hanuman searched everywhere, but to no avail.

Perhaps it was Mahadeva's lila that aimed to teach a lesson in humility to the world, through Hanuman. Or perhaps, it was a reminder that every action, however skilfully executed, required the blessing of Bhagavan, the karma-phala-daata, the giver of fruits of all actions.

Hanuman realized that his efforts fell short. He sat down and fervently prayed to Shiva for guidance.

In Gandhamadana, time was running out. Sita and Rama's entourage had arranged for the puja materials. Now, their eyes frequently turned to the clouds searching for Hanuman. As they waited, Sita started playing with the sand, sculpting it into a linga. This inspired others to follow suit. Soon, the shore was adorned with lingas made by Lakshmana, Jambavan, Nala, Nila, Angada, and the accompanying Vibheeshana.

By then, the muhurtam—the auspicious time—was about to end. But Hanuman had not yet returned.

Concerned about missing the time, the sages suggested, "O Rama, time is running out for the puja. Something must be delaying Hanuman. Janaki's sand linga is appropriate for the puja. Please, do not delay further."

Heeding their counsel, Rama did the *pratistha* of the linga. He shot his arrow, piercing the ground and a jet of water welled up from the ground for ablutions. This small well came to be called Kotiteertha. Rama performed heartfelt worship to Mahadeva and Amba, seeking atonement for his brahma hatya.

Shiva appeared with Amba. "O Rama, the greatest sins will be absolved for all who bathe in the sea at Dhanushkodi and worship this linga, which will henceforth be called Ramalinga or Rameshwara." Rama prostrated to Mahadeva, thankful for the absolution.

Barely had this transpired that Hanuman returned, carrying the Swayambhu Linga from Kailasha. As he observed the scene before him, Hanuman's disappointment was palpable. The revered and feared warrior felt his heart break. He fell under the spell of abject dejection.

He lamented. "I brought this linga from Kailasha with the blessing of Mahadeva and Amba. But it is of no use to you now. What use is this body if it couldn't serve you? I feel like a burden on this earth." He continued, surprising everyone, "Your actions have brought me grief, O Lord, I should abandon this body that you have slighted," he said, prostrating to Rama.

Rama's heart ached, witnessing the warrior's desolation. However, he had to clear Hanuman of this illusory sorrow.

"Dear Hanuman, our body will perish in its own time. The Atman is the eternal truth. Why claim actions as yours or mine? Your action is mine, and my action is yours. Why do you see a difference? Actions follow Ishwara's will, alone." Rama explained the great philosophy of the Upanishads.

Rama lifted Hanuman by his shoulders. "Hanuman, the linga you brought is invaluable. Install it here. It will be known as Vishwa Linga or Hanumat Ishwara. In fact, all devotees will worship Hanumat Linga before praying to Ramalinga."

That solution should have sufficed, but Hanuman sought to replace the sand linga with the one he brought. He was in thrall of his ego.

Rama watched with amusement as he put his hands around the Rameshwara Linga, tugging at it. When a linga is installed with great devotion, it pierces through the seven worlds. Everyone stared in anticipation as Hanuman pulled the linga, first lightly and then with all his might. He circled it, trying to push and tug. Surprised at the difficulty, he looped his tail around the linga, and with a reverberating grunt, pulled it with both arms and his tail, exerting his entire strength.

This monumental effort flung him into the skies. Rama, Sita, and the others looked up in panic as they saw Hanuman fall to the ground a few kilometres to the north. The impact of his fall had created a deep crater. They ran to him and found him unconscious and severely bruised.

Rama wept, recalling the numerous ways in which Hanuman had cared for him. He bemoaned, "O Hanuman, you discovered my beloved Sita. Without you by my side, I would have failed in my fight against the powerful rakshasas. Why did you let the linga become a source of grief? Wake up, Maruti!"

Rama's tears not only revived his consciousness but also removed his ignorance. Remorseful for his foolish actions born of ego, he sought Rama and Sita's forgiveness. "You have dispelled my illusion, my Lord. Mahadeva decides which linga is installed when and where. I foolishly became attached to my actions. The ego is an ever-present foe. I lost vigilance."

Rama embraced him, urging Hanuman to install the linga he brought from Kailasha at that spot, and worship it to appease Mahadeva. "This place where you fell will be named after you—the Hanuman Kunda. People who worship here will gain unwavering knowledge of the Atman."

The kshetram was enriched by the various lingas and they continue to be worshipped today. Great mahatmas and warriors have visited this sacred place to atone for their sins and gain knowledge.

Śrītāmraparṇījalarāśiyōgē nibadhya sētuṁ viśikhairasaṅkhyaiḥ |
śrīrāmacandrēṇa samarpitaṁ taṁ rāmēśvarākhyaṁ niyataṁ namāmi |

I meditate with devotion to the lord of Rama,
who lives in the confluence of river Tamraparni with the sea,
where a bridge was been built with the help of umpteen
arrows of Sri Rama Chandra.
(*Dwadasha Jyotirlinga Stotram*, Adi Shankaracharya)

Rama founded the pan-Bharatiya Yatra tradition. As articulated in the Adhyatma Ramayana, he states, "One should bathe in the sea, behold Rameshwar Mahadev, and thereafter go to Kashi to fetch Ganga water. Offering the Ganga water to Rameshwar Mahadev, they should cast the pot into the sea. This ensures salvation."

This sacred pilgrimage has now been practised for millennia. Over time, Puri in the east and Dwaraka in the west joined Kashi and Rameshwaram, evolving into the revered Char Dham Yatra observed by countless Hindus today.

Sources: Setu Mahatmya, *Skanda Purana*; and Kotirudra Samhita, *Shiva Purana*

Fig. 22.1 An early 20th-century vintage poster narrating the Rameshwara episode from Modern Litho Works

23

Nageshwara

Darukaa, wife of the demon Daruka, was a devotee of Devi Parvati. She regularly worshipped Devi. Touched by Darukaa's unwavering dedication, Parvati gave her a peculiar boon. "Darukaa, your devotion pleases me. I grant you the boon that this entire forest will accompany you wherever you go."

This strange boon puzzled Darukaa. However, believing that Devi must have her reasons, she gratefully accepted the boon. She returned to her husband and his malevolent hordes, who were engaged in tormenting the innocent and righteous. Daruka had ensnared countless people, imprisoning them in the forest.

The tormented innocents in the area beseeched Rishi Aurva for help. Rishi Aurva invoked his tapas and blessed them, "Whoever hurts you will be hurt as well. Whoever kills you will be killed as well." This blessing deterred the rakshasas from continuing their murderous lifestyle.

Seizing this opportune lull, the devas prepared to annihilate the entire clan of rakshasas. Daruka realized the imminent threat to his armies and sought the council of his astute wife, Darukaa.

Darukaa recollected her boon from Parvati. "Natha, I now realize the purpose of the boon Devi gave me. I have the power to transport this entire forest to the ocean. In this way, we can protect ourselves from the devas." Daruka found solace in her suggestion. Darukaa plunged into the western oceans, ferrying the entire Darukavana along with her. The rakshasas rejoiced at their escape.

Yet their proclivity for violence persisted. They captured and plundered merchant ships and fishing boats that crossed the sea from present day Gujarat westward. They imprisoned the sailors in their underwater forest. Countless men were captured in this manner.

Years passed in a relentless cycle of violence until the day they captured a devout Shiva bhakta, the Vaishya merchant Supriya. Supriya was never without the bhasma on his forehead or the Shiva mantra in his heart. He too was dragged to the prison, his precious rudraksha mala dangling from his neck.

Even in captivity, Supriya continued his worship. He fashioned a Shiva Linga out of the mud and began his simple but devoted worship of the Lord. He transformed the prison into an ashram, imparting the glory of Mahadeva to the other prisoners. He regaled them with Mahadeva's stories, initiating them into the Shiva mantra japa, and leading them in daily Shiva puja.

Infuriated upon learning of this burgeoning Shiva bhakti movement, Daruka decided to execute Supriya and squash the growing hope in the prison. His sword was poised to strike. Supriya unblinkingly surrendered to Sadashiva.

Before Daruka's sword descended, a dazzling light emanated from a crevice in the prison. Mahadeva manifested as a column of light, blinding the rakshasas. He bestowed the Pashupata astra upon Supriya, who then fought and vanquished Daruka.

Darukaa, Daruka's wife, implored Parvati for clemency. Parvati, in turn, beseeched Shiva to spare Darukaa and her sons. Shiva smiled at this maternal plea and granted her request. "Darukaa shall be spared. But time will devour her too."

Furthermore, Mahadeva blessed Darukavana, turning it into a sacred site, with the Nageshwar Jyotirlinga temple on its outskirts. Soon, rishis flocked to the forest, settling there. They performed yagnas and tapas, thus sanctifying the once-infamous domain.

That was not the last blessing of Mahadeva in Darukavana. Eons later, he returned in the form of the seductive youth, Bhikshatana, to teach the rishis that mere mechanical performance of rituals would not lead to lasting bliss (refer to chapter on Bhikshatana)

Yāmyē sadaṅgē nagarē'tiramyē
vibhūṣitāṅgaṃ vividhaiścha bhōgaiḥ ।
sadbhaktimuktipradamīśamēkaṃ
śrīnāganāthaṃ śaraṇaṃ prapadyē ॥

I seek refuge of Lord Naganatha,
Who lives in the pretty town
Of Sadanga in the southern part,
Who is well decorated,

Who grants all kinds of pleasures,
And who is the only God who grants,
Devotion and salvation.
(*Dwadasha Jyotirlinga Stotram*, Adi Shankaracharya)

Source: Kotirudra Samhita, *Shiva Purana*

24

Nandikesha

Rishi Shilada was desperate for a son to continue his lineage and offer pindas for his forefathers. However, he did not want his son to be born from a womb and be a mortal. He prayed to Indra for years.

Indra's voice reverberated from the heavens. "Your request is impossible, Shilada. But there is One who has the power to make anything possible. Pray to Mahadeva."

With renewed vigour, Shilada engaged in intense penance, focusing his entire being on Shiva. When Shiva appeared, Shilada was overcome with joy at the sight of that three-eyed divine face and matted locks.

He prostrated before Shiva and said, "Bhagavan, I prayed to you for a son, one who is not be born from a womb and who will be free from death. However, after witnessing your majestic beauty, I have one more request. I want a son like you. Please bless me with such a progeny."

Shiva chuckled at this audacious request. "I cannot create someone like me. Instead, I shall manifest as your son. Go home and perform a yagna. I will emerge from it," Shiva blessed.

Shilada performed a yagna as Shiva had instructed, and from it emerged a child radiant with the effulgence of

Mahadeva. Upon entering his home, however, the divine appearance receded, revealing a normal human child.

Yet the divinity in him remained conspicuous. He grew into a handsome, intelligent, devout youth. He was named Nandi, the one who radiated joy. They performed his *upanayanam* at an early age and raised him as a great scholar and bhakta.

However, tragedy struck soon. Once, Rishis Maitra and Varuna visited the family. As the young boy prostrated before them, their serene faces grew anguished. With their yogic vision, they sensed Nandi's premature demise. Upon enquiring about their sorrow, they revealed their premonition with him. Shilada was heartbroken.

Surprisingly, young Nandi was undaunted. "Mahadeva's boon cannot go wrong. I shall undertake intense tapas so that Shiva is compelled to protect me," he said, setting out for the forest.

After years of penance, Shiva and Uma appeared before Nandi. Mahadeva lifted his right arm into the Abhaya mudra, assuring protection. "O Nandi, you are inseparable from me, my own son. You shall be free from old age and death." Uma, pleased with gaining another son, witnessed the divine reunion.

As Nandi prostrated at their feet, Mahadeva raised him up and embraced him, infusing Nandi with great spiritual wisdom. He relinquished all desires except the longing for Shiva jnana—the knowledge of Shiva.

He spoke words of wisdom. "Lord, eternal life devoid of you is futile and joyless. Please bless me that I may serve you for the rest of my life." He requested.

Shiva was pleased. He said, "The best way to be near me is to be my attendant and leader to my ganas. This is not an easy task. You must deal with my prolonged meditation, my sudden projects to help my devotees, and my unexpected rages. You must lead the Bhuta and Preta ganas with firmness. You must receive rishis and munis and host them reverently. Do you want this role?"

Overjoyed by this honour, Nandi, the son of Shilada prostrated to Shiva. The Shiva ganas were thrilled with their new commander.

Uma-Maheshwara organized the wedding of their new son with Suyasa, the beautiful daughter of the Maruts, the wind gods. Through their marriage, Nandi attained the power of the winds, enabling him to become the vahana of Mahadeva.

Henceforth, Nandi, always by his side, faithfully served Shiva with diligence and wisdom.

shailAdo hi mahAtejA gaNashreShTha purAtanaH|
buddhimAnniti nipuNo mahAbala parAkrami||

He, the son of Shilada, is of great splendor, the chief of the Ganas, and ancient.
He is intelligent, efficient, powerful, and valorous.
(Kedara Khanda, verse 59, Maheshwara Khanda, *Skanda Purana*)

In numerous temples, an endearing tradition involves devotees whispering their prayers in the ears of Nandikeshwara. He ensures that their supplications reach Shiva while he meditates.

Nandi Bhagavan sits majestically facing the Lord, often eclipsing the Shiva Linga in size and grandeur. While Nandi is usually depicted as a seated bull facing Shiva, sometimes he is also shown standing majestically as Adhikara Nandi, the head of all Shiva ganas.

Nandi, true to his name, imparts the knowledge of establishing a connection with the ever-changeless Parabrahman, the source of all joy. Not only is the bull strong and powerful, but he is also a simple, common animal, demonstrating Lord Shiva's simplicity and, as Pashupatinath, his connection to the common people and their animals. From an ecological perspective, the reverence for Nandi translates to respect and care for all bulls across India. The iconography of Nandi with Shiva can be traced as far back as the seals excavated from the Indus Valley. And his presence still endures across Shiva temples.

Nandikeshwara, a guru for both the Shiva Vidya and Sri Vidya traditions, learned them from Devi Parvati and imparted this knowledge to great munis like Patanjali, Vyaghrapada, and Tirumular. That teaching tradition continues until today.

One of his unique roles is playing mridangam for Shiva Tandava. He alone, the amsha of Nataraja, can manage that daunting task.

Source: Satarudra Samhita, chapter 6: "The Incarnations of Nandiswara", *Shiva Purana*

The *Linga Purana, Skanda Purana* and *Vayu Purana* have slightly different stories about Nandi. Initially, Nandikeshwara was the head of the Shiva Ganas. There is no indication that he was a bull. Over time, Nandikeshwara and the Rishabha have been conflated and Nandikeshwara has become both the Rishabha vahana and the head of Shiva Ganas.

Fig. 24.1 Nandi at Chamundi Hills, Mysuru, Karnataka, created during the reign of Dodda Devaraja Wodeyar, the maharaja of Mysuru, 1659–1673
Photo: Karnataka.com

25

Atma Linga

In the 8th century, Pusalar, a Tamil saint, harboured an ardent desire to build a magnificent Shiva temple in his hometown, Tirunindravur. Lacking the financial means, he resorted to building an imaginary temple in his mind. No monetary resources were required for such a mind temple.

This was no casual undertaking for Pusalar. He went through the detailed process of building the temple in his mind with meticulous dedication. For several months, he executed his well-thought-out project plan, as one would for constructing any physical edifice. He selected a serene location, performed the bhumi puja and broke ground on an auspicious day. He diligently studied various temple architectures and designed the layout. He even visualized buying supplies carefully—stones, wood, and tools. He hired architects and builders. He supervised the construction and participated in the labour every day. Gradually, the temple rose in his mind, the foundation, the base plinth, the trims, the pillars, the gopurams, and finally the vimanas. In his imagination, he commissioned gifted sculptors to craft captivating vigrahas of the Lord, Devi Parvati, Ganapati, Nandikeshwara, and all the other devatas. He bedecked them with silken clothes and golden ornaments encrusted with diamonds and gems.

His unwavering focus persisted throughout the day, for months until, one morning, the temple stood complete, in his mind. Eager to consecrate his mind temple, Pusalar consulted his village astrologer, the jyotisha, for an auspicious date for the kumbhabhishekam.

Simultaneously, the Pallava King Rajasimha was constructing a grand Shiva temple in Kanchipuram. He had invested substantial resources engaging the finest architects and sculptors. He intended it to be his legacy. When King Rajasimha planned his temple's *kumbhabhishekam*, his jyotisha proposed the same date and time as that of Pusalar's mind temple.

Rajasimha, preoccupied with pride and excitement about his new temple, found himself unable to sleep. As he dozed off, Shiva appeared in his dream. "I am pleased with your magnificent temple. However, I cannot attend the consecration of your temple as it coincides with another. I must go to Thiruninravur for the kumbhabhishekam of the temple built by my devotee Pusalar."

Such is the omnipresent Mahadeva's lila that he pretended to have a time conflict.

The king awoke from this dream quite perplexed. He rubbed his eyes, wondering, "Who is this Pusalar who has built such a grand temple that Ishwara would go there, forsaking mine?"

Kindled with curiosity, he had his men thoroughly search Thiruninravur. But no new temple was found there. He visited the village himself and gathered the brahmanas. "Tell me truly. Where is the temple built by the devotee Pusalar?"

The brahmanas replied, "There is no such temple. However, there is a devout bhakta named Pusalar in this town." The king rushed to meet this bhakta.

The king asked Pusalar, "Mahadeva informed me that you are building a temple for him. Where is this temple? It must be extraordinary, for Paramashiva committed to attend the kumbhabhishekam at your temple instead of mine."

As Pusalar, immersed in mental preparation for the mental kumbhabhishekam of the mental temple, started sobbing, the truth unfolded.

Overwhelmed, he explained the situation to King Rajasimha. "I have built no real temple. I have no money for even a brick. I have merely imagined the grandest temple in my heart for my Lord and worship him there with all my love. Despite its intangibility, Shiva considers it as real as your grand structure. He is both the greatest and the simplest of them all. Mahadeva is, indeed, Karunamurti, the embodiment of compassion."

The King was astonished by this revelation. Pusalar's bhakti had moved him. He had this incident inscribed in the Kailasanathar temple. This temple is still in Kanchipuram, maintained by the Archaeological Society of India.

To fulfil Pusalar's dream, the King built a temple in that village. This temple, aptly called Hridayaleeswara, the one who resides in the heart, endures still.

Pusalar demonstrated that the poorest bhakta can invoke the Lord in the most sublime temple of all—the human minds. He is not alone. This truth is resonated in the writings of several devotees across time.

The great Kannnada saint of the Veerashaiva tradition, Basaveshwara, emphatically states that built temples may fall, but the moving temples (the human hearts) will never perish.

ullavaru shivalaya maaduvaru naanena maadali badavanayya,
enna kaale kamba dehave degula shirave honna kalashavayya
Koodala Sangama Deva kelayya sthavarakkalivuntu
jangamakalivilla

The rich can build Shivalaya. I am a poor man; what can I do?
My legs are the pillars, my body is the temple,
My head is the wonderful dome.
O lord! Things standing will fall someday; those moving will never!!
(Vachana of Basaveshwara)

Bhagavan Adi Shankara worships this Atma Linga with a series of metaphors.

ārādhayāmi maṇisaṁnibhamāmaliṅgam
māyāpurihṛdayapaṅkajasaṁniviṣṭam
śraddhānadīvimalaīcittajalābhiṣekaih
nityaṁ samādhikusumairnapunarbhavāya ||

I worship daily the precious linga that is the same as my Atma.
I place it in the illusory, lotus-like city of my heart.
I perform abhishekam with my pure thoughts
Drawn from the river of my shraddha.
I offer the flowers of my samadhi.

By doing this, I will be released from the cycle of
birth and death.
(*Nirguna Manasa Puja*, Adi Shankaracharya)

Tirumoolar, the great Tamil siddha, has a similar experience.

Ullam Perungkoil Oonudambaalayam
Vallal Piraanaarkku Vaai Gopuravaasal
Thellath Thelindhaarkkuch Seevan SivaLinga
Kallap Pulanaindhum Kaalaa Manivilakkae.

My heart is the sannidhi (sanctum), and my physical body is
the temple.
Of the compassionate Lord.
My mouth is the entry gopura.
For the purest, the jeeva is the ShivaLinga.
The five errant senses
are the lighted lamps.
(*Thirumandhiram*—Thirumoolar)

These saints reiterate that the Shiva in our hearts is far more vibrant, powerful, and accessible than the Shiva lingas and murtis in any temple, however holy, great, or ancient they may be!

Source: *Kailashanatha Temple* (Kanchipuram) *Sthala Puranam* and *Pusalar Nayanar Puranam* (Periya Puranam Tamil canon)

Acknowledgements

It is purely by the grace of gurus that even a sliver of Shiva bhakti comes to us—prostrations to my gurus and acharyas for their invaluable blessings.

My gratitude is due to my parents for exposing me early on to Shiva sthalas and stories of Shiva and Shaiva saints. It is also a blessing to have my husband and three children join me in my Shiva yatra and be a captive audience for my frequent storytelling.

Thanks to friends who motivated me to publish my scattered blogs as a book. Special mention must be made of Harikiran Vadlamani of Indic Academy and my author-friends Ami Ganatra and Aditi Banerjee Malakar for their support.

I offer immense thanks to the great sadhakas who maintain and contribute to the following rich websites and forums, which made research very easy: Wisdomlib.org, ValmikiRamayan.net, Shodhganga, StackExchange.com, Sanskritdocuments.org, Kamakoti.org, and Wikipedia.org.

It is a blessing for a debut author like me to have the support of Praveen Tiwari and Thanglenhao Haokip of BluOne Ink.

Ultimately, it is Mahadeva Himself who causes His stories to be read, contemplated upon, and shared over eons through different voices. To be one such voice is His ultimate grace.

Glossary

Abhishekam: a type of worship by pouring liquids on the murti (idol)

Ahuti: sacrificial offerings carried to the devas by the fire god Agni

Amrita: the divine ambrosia that was churned from the milky ocean to bestow immortality

Arghyam: water offered to wash hands

Astra: weapons, usually arrows

Asuras: sons and descendants of Rishi Kashyapa and Diti, often clamouring for power in rivalry with the devas

Bhasma: sacred ash that adorns Shiva, also worn by Shiva devotees on their foreheads and arms, symbolizing the inevitability of death of the body

Devas: sons of Rishi Kashyapa and Aditi, beings in charge of running the world

Gandharva: celestial beings known for their expertise in music and dance

Jeeva/Jiva: individual beings who are reborn in new bodies based on their karmas

Jnana: knowledge, usually spiritual knowledge

Jnani: one endowed with the highest knowledge of God and of the self

Kailasha: the celestial abode of Shiva and Parvati, believed to be Mt Kailash in Nepal

Katha: ancient stories in the Itihasas (historical), Puranas (allegorical), Sthala Puranas (temple legends), etc.

Kshetram: a holy abode

Lila: divine play that may appear excessive or controversial but results in universal good and teaches values

Murti: "idols" sculpted according to scriptures in which the deities are invoked and worshiped

Pancha Bhuta: the five elements (sky, air, fire, water, and earth)

Panchakshari: the five-syllable mantra invoking Shiva (Na-ma-Shi-va-ya)

Parikrama: circumambulation of a sacred murti, mountain, or a temple

Prajapati: first mind-born sons of Brahma designated to populate the universe

Pralaya: the dissolution of the universe at the end of each kalpa (4.32 billion years)

Pranava: the name of Om, the primordial sound that is the basis for the Vedas and creation itself

Rudraksha: "Eye of Rudra", essentially dried seeds of the Elaeocarpus tree, often worn by Shiva's devotees

Sapta rishis: a set of seven ancient sages who started civilization

Shakti: divine power

Siddhis: powers gained through penance and sacrifices

Sthala: the holy abode of a deity

Stotram or stuti: a hymn in praise of a deity

Tapas: penance

Tattvam: the deep, subtle concept behind a thing

Vasuki: the king of serpents, son of Rishi Kashyapa and Kadru, who adorns the neck of Shiva

Vigraha: an "idol" sculpted according to scriptures in which the deity is invoked and worshiped

Vivaha: wedding

Yagna: a Vedic sacrifice, usually done to achieve some individual or societal goal

Yagnashala: the sacred place where a yagna is conducted

Yojana: a measurement of distance

About the Author

Deepa Bhaskaran Salem is a student of Hindu dharma and Advaita Vedanta. She speaks and writes on Hindu dharma, Itihasas, Puranas, Bhagavad Gita, parenting, and mental health in popular platforms and her own blog. She also conducts workshops for children and adults with insights drawn from Sanatana Dharma.

She has been a management consultant and marketing leader. She currently runs a technology marketing consultancy in the United States.

Guided by her gurus, she is on a journey to achieve the bliss of Shiva—Shivananda.

www.ingramcontent.com/pod-product-compliance
Lightning Source LLC
Chambersburg PA
CBHW071324150526
44903CB00047B/1139
* 9 7 8 9 3 9 2 2 0 9 9 1 8 *